U-Boat War

LOTHAR-GÜNTHER BUCHHEIM
U-BOAT WAR

Translated by Gudie Lawaetz
and with an Essay by Michael Salewski

Bonanza Books . New York

Translation Copyright © MCMLXXVIII by Alfred A. Knopf, Inc.
Copyright © MCMLXXVI by R. Piper & Co. Verlag GmbH, Zurich

Originally published in Germany under the title *U-Boot-Krieg*.

This 1986 edition is published by Bonanza Books, distributed by Crown
Publishers, Inc., by arrangement with Alfred A. Knopf, Inc.

Printed and Bound in the United States of America

Library of Congress Cataloging in Publication Data

Buchheim, Lothar-Günther.
   U-boat war.

   Translation of: U-Boot-Krieg.
   Reprint. Originally published: New York : Knopf,
1978.
   1. World War, 1939-1945—Naval operations—Submarine.
2. World War, 1939-1945—Naval operations, German.
3. World War, 1939-1945—Campaigns—Atlantic Ocean.
I. Salewski, Michael. II. Title.
D781.B7813   1986   940.54′51   86-2275
ISBN 0-517-60671-2

h g f e d c b a

All of the photographs in this book were taken by Lothar-Günther
Buchheim, with the exception of those of the torpedo strike on a
freighter, which were taken by Fritz Grade, Directing
Engineer of U-Boat 96.

Contents

From a long and miserable experience of suffering, injustice, disgrace, and aggression the nations of the earth are mostly swayed by fear—fear of the sort that a little cheap oratory turns easily to rage, hate, and violence. Innocent, guileless fear has been the cause of many wars. Not, of course, the fear of war itself, which, in the evolution of sentiments and ideas, has come to be regarded at last as a half-mystic and glorious ceremony with certain fashionable rites and preliminary incantations, wherein the conception of its true nature has been lost.

             —Joseph Conrad

I struggled in the beginning. I said I was going to write the truth so help me God. And I thought I was. I found I couldn't. Nobody can write the absolute truth.

             —Henry Miller

U-Boat War

The Experience of Submarine War

The submarine has given man a new dimension—the depths of the sea. The realm of the pilot is very different from that of the submarine captain, but both aircraft and submarine are part of man's endeavor to escape his earthbound state.

Every ship, down to the meanest trawler and the tiniest skiff, radiates something of the miracle inherent in any voyage across the oceans: man's domination of an alien element. But the submarine is supreme among vessels. The submarine has overcome humanity's ancient dread of the sea, for it can penetrate the sea's depths without fear of destruction.

Normal ships live out their lives on the surface of the waters. The water they displace with their rounded bellies provides them with buoyancy. Whenever that is lost they go under, sucked down into the chasm. A ship deprived of its buoyancy cannot regain it. It is struck off the list of living vessels, aground, missing, gone.

The moment of sinking is every sailor's lifelong nightmare, because it means the death of ship and crew. But for the men aboard a submarine, sinking is part of normal seamanship.

The submarine alone can recover its buoyancy after disappearing from the surface, thanks to its intricate system of highly developed machinery. When the air stored in steel compression tanks rushes into the ballast tanks, forcing water out, the submarine is made lighter than the water it displaces, is lifted up and can rise to the surface to become once again a ship supported by the waves, able to endure the rigors of wind and weather.

For a normal surface vessel the slightest contact with the seabed is a constant terror. (Joseph Conrad is the poet of all the humiliations of this predicament.) It has always been a captain's prime concern to keep his ship from running aground.

But for a submarine, touching bottom is a practiced routine. In waters whose depth does not exceed its diving limits, it can lie on the seabed and rest its engines. Its own weight and that of the water in the trim cells holds it steadier and more securely than the strongest anchor.

Aboard a submarine, therefore, the sailor need no longer fear being mauled by the winds or the waves—and yet he remains subject to the laws of Nature. Indeed, the rules by which he must now abide are even more complicated. The captain of a submarine has to be acquainted with physics, with chemistry, with engineering. He must be as alert and as observant of the rules as any of his forebears on the sailing ships of old, who were warned of approaching danger by a soft rustle of sails or an almost imperceptible change in the color of the sky. Despite all its technical perfection, the submarine, too, requires unceasing watchfulness.

Unlike the normal ship, the submarine does not sail toward harbor. Its destination is enemy shipping; in the last war that shipping had to be stalked in the immensity of the Atlantic. Though the older captains would never think of these enemy ships, even in wartime, except as living creatures of steel, the chatter of propaganda went farther and turned them into abstractions. Nothing was said of the men serving aboard them or of the cargoes they carried. The sinking reports, which determined the handout of medals, did not even differentiate between loaded and empty ships—nothing counted but the tonnage. Reading or listening to the texts emanating from the Ministry of Propaganda, many a submarine captain must have imagined himself the employee of some vast scrap metal business.
The trumpeting of endless gross registered tons (how many of those listening to the radio had any idea of what exactly a gross registered ton might be?) was intended to blur reality and to fan the ominous "Will to Win."
Nor did the war correspondents give anyone a clear picture of what was really involved in convoy battle: over a distance of thousands of miles, as days and nights stretched into weeks, steamers were pursued, submarines were annihilated under water, and the stench of burning tankers filled the air above a trail of wreckage, lifeboats, and floating cargo. A stranglehold of fear reached across the Atlantic, covering it like a gigantic invisible dome of glass: tempted aboard the freighters by high pay, thousands of sailors, many of them well past their prime, now sweated out their fear of torpedoes. And aboard the submarines thousands "killed their pants"—the euphemism for fear in German naval slang—at the mere thought of attacks by the "hunter-killer groups" made up of destroyers and aircraft.

The fascination of the submarine and the prestige of the submarine service run counter to grim reality: because it is invisible the submarine is treacherous. Its torpedoes are like animated, self-propelled mines. Almost invariably, it is the captain's intention to hit an adversary unawares.
The submarine is simultaneously a ship and a weapon—and as such it was the symbol of our own schizophrenia: we were bound for adventure and for destruction.
Way back then, in the bunker pens of the French Atlantic coast, fascinated beyond measure and with Joseph Conrad in my heart, I devoured the sensuous perfection of the submarines with my eyes the way a rider worships the lines of his horse.
But when, many years after the war, I heard a submarine captain's widow delightedly exclaim, "Dear little boat!" as she was leafing through an album

of old photos and came upon some pictures of the fighting VII-C, I was utterly appalled: this seaborne marauding engine of war was never, ever, a "dear little boat."

And when I read the sentence by my reviewer Donald Goddard in the *New York Times* of June 29, 1975, that of the 40,000 men who had gone forth as volunteers in German submarines to wage total war against innocent civilians, the 30,000 dead had fully deserved their dreadful fate at sea, I was incensed by the coldbloodedness of the verdict. However horrific the idea that these young men, lured into action by every form of propaganda, came very close to bringing down an empire, it is not the individual sent to his doom that merits such merciless condemnation.

As a twenty-three-year-old artist, my part in reporting the war was to produce suitable paintings and drawings. I was not a war photographer—what pictures I shot were for my own record. Convinced that the reality of the war was not being reflected in the routine dispatches of war correspondents, I was driven to take more than five thousand photos. Every aspect, every detail counted, bore witness to the reality of war, for unless I captured it on film it was irretrievably gone. Perhaps it was a kind of protest against such terrible transience that impelled me to almost manic lengths to capture images—a determination to render an account of everything we did and endured.

Indeed, when hopes of survival, of the chance to bear witness, began to dwindle in the final year of the war, when everything really did "come crashing down in smithereens," in the words of the song we used to sing, I took up the camera less and less frequently.

Most of these photos I rediscovered only recently on timeworn, battered reels of undeveloped film I had lost sight of long ago. When I fished the sodden enlargements out of the bath, I was suddenly conscious that what I was holding were historical documents, most of them thirty-five years old.

If I want these pictures to be seen, it is because a new generation has grown up for whom the events depicted are not part of their own experience, but "History," something historians can describe but not evoke, not conjure up visually.

The U-boats of World War II: they exemplify all the claustrophobia, the constriction, and the oppression of the period.

For those of my generation, these pictorial documents will, I trust, be a reminder of what it was like.

Occupation—The Atlantic Bases

France capitulated in June of 1940. Control of the French Atlantic ports decisively altered Germany's strategic naval situation. The string of bases at the Navy's disposal now stretched from the Arctic Sea to the Bay of Biscay. The age-old handicap of having to operate exclusively out of the "liquid triangle" of the North Sea was thus removed. The enemy could no longer lie in ambush as German ships departed or bar their way home, as had been possible in Operations Elbe and Jade.

Recognition of the strategic advantages gained with the occupation of France induced the Naval High Command on June 18, 1940, to formulate their military demands as follows: "The capitulation of France must result not merely in the elimination of French forces from the present struggle, but must also be exploited in every possible way for the continuation of war against England. . . ."

This command was gradually implemented. Beyond the strategic use to which the occupied territories were put, the economic resources of France were systematically exploited. Workers were forced into slave labor through the bureaucratic device known as *Dienstverpflichtung*—"service commitment." Agriculture and industry were incorporated into the supply structure of the German Reich.

The subjugation of France was complete. There were remarkably few conflicts. A resigned acceptance of the occupation and of the ubiquity of foreign uniforms in the streets of occupied cities fed German hubris daily.

"Out of regard for the German people, we have to make certain that the French are not let off scot-free because of any misguided sentimentality on our part. Time and again we must make it absolutely clear that negotiations are out of the question until we have a firm hold on France's Army, Navy, and weaponry, and that for the next three or four hundred years France will have no further opportunity to launch an unprovoked attack against a peaceful people." (Goebbels, June 18, 1940)

A Conquered Nation

Initially, the German authorities tried to persuade the French by means of inducements and privileges to work voluntarily for the occupation forces. As time went on, the measures grew harsher: a decree dated February 16, 1943, imposed two years of obligatory service on all French men and women born between January 1, 1920, and December 31, 1922. An executive order dated January 13, 1943, emanating from Hitler personally, decreed the com-

Paris, Place de la Concorde. The Guards Regiment, which marches to the Arc de Triomphe, day in day out, in order to humiliate the French.

prehensive mobilization of both men and women for a variety of tasks in the defense of occupied territories.

A law dated February 1, 1944, extended the application of a previous one dating back to September 4, 1942: all men between the ages of sixteen and sixty, and all women aged eighteen to forty-five, could thereafter be drafted to serve the Germans in the so-called *Arbeitsdienst*—it was no more and no less than slave labor.

The U-boat crews soon felt thoroughly at ease in France, which was to them a kind of paradise. Later on, when German cities were succumbing to Allied bombardment in a mass of rubble and ashes, the crews were no longer sent home on leave but were ordered instead to French "submarine pastures," where their superiors thought they would be safer.

Despite all the pressure they were under, the local people were not particularly hostile in their behavior. Anywhere along the seaboard people are well aware that every sailor's enemy is the sea. The submarine crews were greatly envied by all other detachments of the German Navy, by the men serving on minesweepers and patrol boats, because of the ample privileges they enjoyed as an elite. In order to underline their special status, the submariners liked to call themselves the Dönitz Volunteer Corps.

Lorient was the first German base on the west coast of France, and the first German submarine to turn up there, on July 5, 1940, was the U-30 under Lemp. Soon there was Brest as well, and La Pallice, St.-Nazaire, and Bordeaux. All in all, eight submarine flotillas were stationed at these bases. This considerably increased the range of the U-boats, which were henceforth spared the long haul through the North Sea. They could reach the theater of operations more quickly and thus had more scope for their actual missions.

Disposition of the flotillas was as follows:

Submarine flotilla No. 1 based at Brest.
Submarine flotilla No. 2 based at Lorient.
Submarine flotilla No. 3 based at La Pallice.
Submarine flotilla No. 6 based at St.-Nazaire.
Submarine flotilla No. 7 based at St.-Nazaire.
Submarine flotilla No. 9 based at Brest.
Submarine flotilla No. 10 based at Lorient.
Submarine flotilla No. 12 based at Bordeaux.

On October 19, 1940, the Second Submarine Flotilla put in the following request to the High Command for offices, workshops, and other accommodations:

1. *Operations Offices.*

   Flotilla Commander, Lieutenant Staff Officer, Personal Aide, Administrative Aide, Base Commander, Flotilla Chief Engineer, Second Flotilla Engineer, Third Flotilla Engineer, Medical Officer, Second Medical Officer, Flotilla Administration Officer, Second Flotilla Administration Officer, Third Flotilla Administration Officer, Fourth Flotilla Administration Officer, Unclassified Records Office, Classified Records Office, Regulations Library, Administration—Engineering Dept., Reference Library—Engineering Dept.

   Offices for Submarine Watch Officers (2 rms), Medical Officer's Registry, Consulting Room, Pharmacy, Sickbay, Administrator (2 rms), Paymaster (2 rms), Accounting Office, Paymaster's Registry, Supplies, Guardmaster, Flotilla Chief Navigator's Office, Rations, Mail Room, Artillery Mechanic and Damage Control Officer (1 rm), Torpedo Mechanic (1 rm).

2. *Auxiliary Accommodations.*

   Artillery Workshop, Carpentry Workshop, Torpedo Mechanic's Workshop, Personal Aide's Records Office, Teletype, Projection Room, Mess Hall, 30 Stores, 20 Detention Cells, Garage, Clothing Store, also allow for diving vehicle.

Such bilingual landmarks symbolized the occupation of a vanquished country in the mind of every soldier. This particular specimen was located in La Baule, the French seaside resort near the port of St.-Nazaire. Here the submarine flotillas had their "pastures."

"We went into the war with a tiny submarine force, since the English had astutely asked themselves what danger could someday threaten them from Germany, and singled out the submarine for total ban in the disgraceful treaty of 1918. When war broke out, we proceeded to build a huge submarine force, but naturally that took some time to make operational." (Dönitz, October 8, 1943.)

So that the fighting submarines could be out chasing the enemy for longer periods, they were supplied by submarine tankers in mid-Atlantic with fuel, torpedoes, and provisions. These vessels also served as floating repair shops. Every one of these "sea cows" could deliver up to 432 tons of diesel oil to fighting subs.

Altogether, there were ten such Type-XIV ships. The spectacle of their return to port was not a common one: without exception they were scuttled, one after another in quick succession. They were too clumsy and too slow to be anything but easy prey for aircraft. Usually they were caught in the very process of provisioning. Unless they were actually cruising, they could not dive "dynamically"; that is, they were unable to make a fast descent without the help of surface rudders and hydroplanes (the fore and aft fins which control a submarine's upward and downward motion).

St.-Nazaire was the home port of the Sixth and the Seventh Submarine Flotillas. Unlike the natural harbors of Brest and Lorient, St.-Nazaire (and La Pallice) relied on locks to keep the water level constant within the anchorage. Such locks are particularly delicate spots in any harbor installation.

A Type-VII-C submarine and one of the so-called sea cows (a large submarine tanker) entering the lock at St.-Nazaire. Decorating the tower of the VII-C boat, the emblem of the Seventh Submarine Flotilla, the Bull of Scapa Flow.

The locks, where incoming and outgoing submarines were as defenseless as in open docks, were among the Royal Air Force's favorite targets. But they were rarely hit and the surrounding residential areas suffered the greatest damage. Toward the end of the war, the town of St.-Nazaire had been reduced to a mass of rubble by Allied air raids against shipyards and docks. Its 46,000 inhabitants had fled in all directions.

When the English saw that their bombs were failing to hit the locks, they opted for their famous raid on St.-Nazaire, which at the time so astonished us that we could find no words for it but "mindless" and "completely crazy." The English had a two-fold aim: to paralyze the submarine base and to prevent the battleship *Tirpitz* from making its way into the main lock, the Normandy Lock, which was also a mammoth dock. But the raid was not even halfway successful: their destroyer *Campbeltown* was driven into the lock's gate and scuttled, but the damage was soon repaired—and German U-boats continued to sail unimpeded from St.-Nazaire and returned to base after each mission. The English did, however, only just miss killing off the entire elite of German submarine captains in one fell swoop: very shortly before the cargo of explosives hidden aboard the English destroyer blew up, the captains had all been wandering about on the deck above, resplendent in their snow-white service dress, for all the world like curious tourists.

No air raid shelters were built for the locks until the war was drawing to a close.

Flotilla Rituals

Whenever they returned to base at St.-Nazaire from a mission, unless the tide happened to be high, the submarines moored within the lock.

The men would stand on the upper deck wearing the characteristic submarine gear: garments of gray leather or else gray fatigues. For many of them, this would be the first gasp of fresh air since their departure. Their halting steps, their clumsy movements revealed that they were not yet acclimatized. Bearded, with hollow cheeks and feverish eyes, they would submit with some embarrassment to the ceremonial welcome. The captain would accept whole armfuls of flowers offered by some of the "lightning girls" or "carbolic cookies," and pose for the photographer.

The Flotilla Commander has laid on a party for submarine officers in a nearby country house. Their studiously casual stance is part and parcel of a rigid code of behavior. The enlisted men can be more relaxed: after a few bottles of beer, they can settle down at their ease to have a good time.

Later on, in the mess, the first round of drinks would loosen the captain's tongue: "It's quite something—working on a convoy over a distance of seven hundred miles! And lousy weather all the way. At one point there was a destroyer coming straight for us. Narrowest silhouette you've ever seen. Once again we thought we'd had it. But it hadn't even noticed us. And then the gray nights up there. Faces the color of cheese, the way you look in the moonlight—only there wasn't any moon: those Northern Lights. Then we bagged a tanker sailing all alone. I was beginning to think we'd fired a dud—but then they started hollering on the bridge! The flames went up in a rush three hundred feet at least—every color from white to black-blood-red—one enormous mushroom! The ship looked like a slab of iron in a forge. It's pretty eerie when a ten-thousand-ton barge like that gets blown sky-high. It makes your blood run cold. God, I'd hate to be on board. But then perhaps it's better that way. At least it's all over in one go."

Karl Dönitz, Commander in Chief of Submarines, then Admiral of the Fleet, and finally the Führer's chosen successor, the last head of state of the Greater German Reich—here at the Château of Kernével near Lorient where the staff of the Submarine Division was stationed for a time.

Training flotillas in the Baltic provided a steady flow of "human material." The so-called canoes (left) were used as training vessels. They had proved themselves primarily as minelayers against English seaports. Toward the end of 1939 they were given over to the submarine training schools. In the course of the war the submarine force was rapidly bled white, and crews became younger all the time. Of this situation, Dönitz made the following comment on October 8, 1943: "... We shall have to man the majority of submarines with very young recruits. Youth is no shortcoming, when there is real manhood within. Youth is unencumbered, youth is healthy. But their training must be all the more thorough, and it is all the more important that the quality of human material recruited into the Navy be of the highest."

"The Führer has ordered that the air war against England is to be stepped up aggressively. Priority is to be given to those targets whose demolition would be most likely to disrupt public life. Aside from air strikes against harbor and industrial installations, cities other than London are to be subjected to terror-raids within a general framework of retribution." (Wehrmacht High Command, April 14, 1942.)

"Irreplaceable cultural treasures are being destroyed such as have not been destroyed in any conflict since the Thirty Years' War and on a vaster scale than in any previous war in history. The inevitable result of this is certain to be a boundless hatred between peoples and an obligatory escalation of weaponry on both sides, and this will redound in such annihilation of values in Europe as can only be deplored from the point of view of Western culture. But such considerations cannot be taken into account by the Chiefs of Staff, and so there is no choice but to exact an eye for an eye, a tooth for a tooth." (War diary of Naval Group Command North, April 26, 1942.)

A city after bombardment by the Royal Air Force.

A dead British pilot on French soil.

Preceding pages:
Since the Allies had no dive bombers with improved target sights, they destroyed entire neighborhoods when their goal was a bridge, hit areas of housing when they intended to drop their bombs on harbor installations.

While the sea instantly eliminates all traces of battle, on land the images of destruction are lasting: to the left the remnants of a bombed-out munitions train, to the right a German patrol boat after a direct hit. Below, a shot-down German aircraft.

Flying in close formation, Boeing bombers attack the naval base. Their pilots do not know that naval anti-aircraft batteries have replaced Army ordnance. Therefore they make their approach at their usual level—and fly straight to their doom. Very quickly the naval ordnance scores six hits. The sky is flecked with the gray clouds of explosions, white parachutes and severed wings, which come fluttering down like scraps of paper and look harmless until you hear their malevolent whine. Far too few parachutes. From some aircraft, none is released at all. One man falls like a stone when his parachute fails to open.

Despite a hailstorm of machine-gun fire, soldiers have dragged the pilot from a Boeing bomber that has come down in flames in a pine grove—but this smashed body cannot be restored by any doctor's art.

The Submarines Take Cover

Whenever the submarines returned from a tough mission for repairs in dry dock, they were particularly vulnerable to any air raid against the bases. Indeed, they themselves were the bait which kept attracting wave upon wave of bombers to these ports. With its broad keel up on blocks, wedged in by wooden props on either side, a submarine undergoing repairs is as helpless as a fish on dry land.

Since we did not have the planes to counterattack the Allied bomber squadrons, the only solution was to build cavelike air raid shelters for our extremely vulnerable craft. The building sites for these U-boat bunkers were vast, and veritable termite-swarms of workers were assigned to the task.

To this day it remains unclear why the Allies did not attack these bunkers while they were under construction, when it would have been easy to smash them, but only began bombing them after layers of exceptionally reinforced concrete, up to twenty-five and even thirty feet thick, had been installed, which sheltered them successfully until the very last year of the war. Not a single submarine suffered bomb damage in port after they were built, until late in 1944. Only at the very end did the British manage with their super-bombs to open a single breach in the bunker at Brest.

A report from the naval shipyard at Lorient describes the situation in September 1942:

"In the course of last year, the submarine shelters and their immediate surroundings were subjected to major bombing. They have shown that even bombs weighing up to a thousand kilograms failed to cause any damage to the ceilings. It was undoubtedly correct to fit corrugated iron to the underside of the ceilings, because despite all the steel reinforcement the concrete would otherwise tend to crumble. The armored gates on the land and sea sides have not yet been exposed to any tests of pressure. The effect of bombs in the vicinity of the bunkers has brought us to the point where we shall have to install supplementary accommodations, such as canteens and kitchens, offices, etc., in air raid shelters. It used to be thought that bunker space was far too costly for such purposes. But this point of view has proved erroneous. Recent events have caused me to make arrangements in Lorient for the construction of an additional bunker, which will also house an anti-aircraft battery, and in St.-Nazaire for an expansion of the existing shelter, which houses the heating system. Should we be instructed to increase the number of sheltered berths—in Lorient and Brest as well—I must demand categorically that the bunkers be built some ten to twelve feet higher than hitherto, so that we can construct an extra floor and thus gain sufficient sheltered space for the workers, for all sanitary installations and supplementary premises, for I am still—as I have often stressed—opposed to *any* unsheltered repair work on submarines. A shipyard situated in an area exposed to attack from the air must be general quarters, i.e., not a soul must be visible on deck."

A confrontation between a member of the Todt Organization and French construction workers. The shelters are built by imported hosts of German workers and French forced labor.

Gradually, not only the boats but also the workshops where returning boats were repaired took refuge under concrete, until entire shipyards with all their complicated installations were safely ensconced beneath a thirty-foot layer of protection.

Up on the coffer dam, beyond which the building site for an extension of the shelter is being excavated, huge mounds of rusty-red T-irons lie in readiness. A giant crane lifts a whole pile of these T-irons at a time. Others are already being driven into the ground by mammoth steam pile drivers—one after another, in a circle, until eventually they form great potlike containers. Pipes as thick as a man's thigh are feeding sand into the completed pots from barges which have been filled up by bulldozers out at the mouth of the river. From up in the giant crane, the T-iron pots standing in a semicircle look like the beads of a necklace. Straight-angled walls of T-irons would not do: the pressure of water in the harbor basin is too great. Powerful pumps pour liquid concrete onto the roof of the shelter: in accordance with an order of the Führer's, all shelter roofs are to be reinforced with yet another extra layer. The place where the fastening-irons are being bent looks like a huge arsenal for a regiment of lancers.

The submarines of the VII-C class were about 220 feet long. Their maximum diameter was 20 feet. Their two diesel engines mustered 2,800 horsepower. They could carry 180 tons of fuel for the diesel engines. Fourteen torpedoes could be stowed aboard in the torpedo tubes and in compartments beneath the floor plates. Alternatively, each boat could carry 22 TMC mines, or 44 TMA mines, or 60 TMB mines.

Because it can dive, the submarine is an effective minelayer; it can creep up to the enemy's shores unseen, even in daytime, establish where exactly the traffic of shipping is densest and then place its load of mines. But the submarine's unique weapon is the torpedo. The submarine's mobility, its capacity to dive and to maneuver submerged, come into play during a torpedo attack, and so does its low silhouette, which makes the boat almost invisible as it rides the surface in twilight or at nighttime.

The word "fire" is commonly used in connection with the torpedo—"to fire a torpedo," "a boat has fired all its torpedoes." In fact, the torpedo is not a projectile at all. It is not expelled from the tube by the force of an explosion but by a blast of compressed air. Equipped with an engine, propellers, and a rudder of its own, the torpedo is itself a highly developed unmanned submarine streaking along just below the surface. Its cargo is the explosive charge.

More than 650 boats of the VII-C type were put into service, 691 boats in all being built of Type-VII.

The boat's water displacement was 1,005 cubic yards at the surface and 1,138 cubic yards submerged. Its range of operations was exceptionally wide; namely, 8,850 nautical miles on the surface at 10 knots, 6,500 nautical miles at 12 knots. Submerged, its range was a mere 80 nautical miles at 4 knots. Its maximum speed was 17.3 knots on the surface and 7.6 knots submerged. But at top speed the E-motors (electric motors) quickly exhausted the energy stored in the batteries, and these boats were constantly running the danger of being "starved out" by their pursuers. No specific data were made available regarding battery capacity, because a battery's performance varies too much, depending largely on its age and maintenance (as is the case with automobile batteries). Submerged, a VII-C boat could travel comfortably on one engine at low speed for as long as three days, but when it had both engines running at top speed, it could carry on for no more than approximately two hours. Whenever the "battery juice" ran out, the boat was obliged to surface because it could not remain static at a given depth; it could only hold a position under water dynamically, by activating its rudder and hydroplanes.

Beneath the cutting edge of this VII-C boat's bow, the hawser, the vents, and the slightly opened door of the upper torpedo tube to starboard are clearly visible. The forward hydroplanes are sticking out like fins. To the back of the tower one can make out something of the "conservatory," the anti-aircraft battery's platform, encircled by railings. Both the direction finder and the sky periscope are up.

Though VII-C boats became outdated in the course of the war, they were miraculous masterpieces of shipbuilding and weapons technology. The pressure hull enclosed a confusing profusion of complex machinery: diesel engines and electric motors, ballast tanks, and the torpedo firing mechanisms. Figures provided by the Office for Naval Construction on September 23, 1941, give some idea of the resources in manpower and materials required for constructing such a craft: "For the delivery of one submarine, some 2,400 workers are needed per month, which means 50,400 for twenty-one boats. Another 70 men minimum, or 100 maximum, are needed to equip a submarine once it is built. The calculations which follow are based on an average figure of 85 workers. To equip 300 front-line boats (of which 150 at any given time would be undergoing repairs), a contingent of 85 times 150 = 12,750 workers will be needed in the shipyards. In addition, 63 workers (3 × 21) will be needed to finish and equip the new boats undergoing tests and front-line training and to work on some 65 training vessels. It is estimated that some thirty of these additional boats will require repairs at any one time, which would call for 2,550 additional workers. Thus the total work force required amounts to 50,400 + 12,750 + 2,550 = 65,700. This is a relatively modest figure, bearing in mind that some 136,000 workers, 70 percent of them skilled, are at present (according to figures provided by the Bureau of Ordnance) employed at shipyards (other than FPB and minesweeper shipyards), now working in and outside Germany for the German Navy. Furthermore, it should be remembered that the number of submarines undergoing repairs at the present time is unlikely to have reached 60 (which corresponds to only 5,100 workers), so that the total labor force thus employed does not at this time exceed 55,500. This still leaves 80,500 men for other tasks in the shipyards. The Submarine Division of the Naval High Command argues therefore that, considering the priority status afforded to the submarine building program with a view to prompt destruction of the shipping carrying supplies to England, a destruction in which the submarine today plays and must in our opinion continue to play a predominant part, the corresponding manpower must under all circumstances be made available, particularly since conditions, in terms of raw materials and shipyard facilities, most certainly allow at the present for the construction of 24–25 submarines a month. If it should emerge that the remaining 80,500 workers—together with those additional recruits to the labor force, who to a certain, if inadequate, extent have been made available on a regular basis despite the considerable prevailing difficulties (approximately 30,000 from January 1940 to June 1941) and will presumably be available in future—do not suffice to perform the remaining tasks in the shipyards, it is our view that adjustments and cutbacks must first be made in these other spheres, until such time as it becomes possible to fulfill their requirements too.

"The Submarine Division of the Naval High Command, as the department responsible for assuring the implementation of the submarine program, considers it a duty to state unequivocally what would be the inevitable consequences of any further cutback in the submarine building program—particularly one so drastic as that announced by K (of the Office for Naval Construction). Such a cutback is unacceptable. It would mean that we would have to give up using the submarine as the principal weapon in the struggle against Britain's supply lines, if not an end to the effectiveness of submarine warfare in general."

There are no compartments aboard a submarine, such as you find on surface vessels. Even the customary divisions between the engine room, the hold, and the crew's quarters are absent. The inside of a submarine is rather like an express train carriage with an aisle down the middle and open areas leading off it on either side. Even the "wardroom" has traffic going through all the time. All those coming off or going on guard duty have to squeeze by the officers' mess table, which protrudes sideways into the aisle. The padded bench which seats the captain, an officer of the watch, and the engineer officer at mealtimes is actually the latter's bunk, serving double duty during the day. All paperwork is done atop the selfsame mess table, and that includes coding and decoding radio signals. The "captain's cabin" is no more than a narrow recess separated by a green curtain from the center passage. This niche also serves as his "office." Here the captain writes his war log. Every back rest even has its built-in locker, so that not a single cubic inch goes to waste. When you open a locker door, you come up against pipes and cables painted white and realize that the thin pane of finely grained wood is there merely to camouflage the technical installations, to create the illusion that the designers have indeed taken human needs into account. In fact, the whole thing is nothing but a steel cigar tube crammed with machinery and weapons. Anything not of iron or steel looks totally out of place.

To get back for a moment to human needs. There is only a single toilet for fifty men. A second one does in fact exist, its bulkhead leading straight into the galley, but it is kept crammed with provisions, so that the boat can last yet a little longer out at sea. The only available toilet cannot even be used at all times: not when the boat is submerged at more than eighty-odd feet; and even at less than that, it's a circus act to cope with the intricate machinery.

My bunk is in the petty officers' quarters, the U-room, on the starboard side of the passage leading from the control room back to the galley. When the hatches astern are open, in comes the stench of diesel oil. There are no skylights, no portholes for ventilation.

On either side of the passage there are four built-in bunks. In the middle of the passage, screwed to the floor, there is a table with folding leaves, which can be dropped to right and left, so that people can get by. A compressed air hatch separates the U-room from the control room. All around the bulkhead opening, sausages and slabs of smoked meat are dangling, mixed in with leather gear and oilskins like slovenly decorations in some butcher's window. Thick bundles of cables and pipes run along the ceiling. When you open the locker doors, the sight is the same as in the wardroom: a confusion of pipes, cables, and vents.

Beneath the floor plates of the U-room lies Battery Two, which supplies the engines with energy for running under water, along with tanks for fuel, fresh and dirty water. In all the so-called rooms the floor plates are just about halfway up the pressure hull.

As I lie on my bunk and stare at the curved wall of the pressure hull, I lose my impression of the boat as a deep-sea fish—which is what it looked like in dock. A fish has a skeleton of bones. There is nothing comparable inside the submarine. I feel, rather, like Jonah inside some huge shellfish whose vulnerable parts are sheathed in armor.

My own locker is just about big enough to hold a briefcase. It is possible for the lockers to be that tiny, because nobody lives on board when the sub is in harbor. This, too, distinguishes the submarine from other vessels. It does not provide the crew with a home. Geared exclusively to warfare, it allows the men just enough space to vegetate and to perform essential chores. The sausages dangling from the ceiling even in the control room are grotesque fairground symbols of the human condition, hopelessly lost inside this battle-engine.

Surprising as it sounds, the U-boats of World War II, like the submarines of World War I, were used as surface vessels until almost the very end. Except for the later models of snorkel boats, they should really be called "diving boats": they used to dive only for a submerged attack, or to escape the pursuit of destroyers and corvettes, or when the sea was very rough, or else when visibility was so poor that enemy vessels were easier to locate with the listening gear than binoculars. It is indicative of the real nature of submarines in both world wars that daily diving practice was mandatory in order to establish whether "in an emergency" the boat was even fit to dive at all—ordinarily, "on the march," the subs operated *above* the water level.

But even when it was running on the surface, the U-boat was barely visible to enemy shipping if the sea was at all rough: so little of it protruded that its outline could easily escape notice, unless its course happened to run directly parallel to that of an observer.

The corresponding disadvantage was its low angle of lookout, which gave it a narrow range of vision. On the whole, the submarines needed the help of an extra eye—i.e., aircraft able to scan a wider area. The absence of any combined submarine/air reconnaissance effort in mid-Atlantic (the Germans had no long-range four-engine planes apart from the Condor aircraft based in Bordeaux) was one of the factors which contributed to the ultimate defeat of the German submarine force.

Of the Type-VII-C boat, no less than 691 were put into service. That is probably the biggest series ever built of any warship. The High Command gambled resolutely on massive deployment of a model that had proved its worth, as opposed to risking innovation. Initially, that may have had certain advantages given the submarine "pack" tactics favored by Dönitz—but as the war wore on, such an armaments policy proved disastrous: right up to the end of World War II, German crews had to sail on boats whose outfitting was Spartan compared with any other navy and which were almost indistinguishable in terms of their design and their armaments from their forebears of World War I. Response to the enemy's technical advances came far too late. Nonetheless, an entry in the war log of the High Command, dated July 11, 1941, reads as follows: "... U-boat Headquarters points out that the existing designs can be considered highly satisfactory in every respect, and that they have given rise to no criticism whatsoever from the front. The Navy can be well pleased with the existing models."

The individual boxes within the submarine shelter are so designed that they can be drained and used as dry docks. Inside the shelter the boat looks like a huge beached prehistoric whale. Taken from its natural habitat, its shape is fully exposed: the knife edge of its bow, the expansive line of its rounded belly, which accommodates the diving cells, the hydroplane fins, and the mouthpieces of the torpedo tubes. This photo does not show how the pressure hull narrows fore and aft. Because its cylindrical shape is ill-suited to surface travel, it is encapsulated within a second skin shaped rather more like an ordinary ship, which supports a narrow upper deck. This outer casing is not pressure-proof, which is why it is pierced by numerous vents through which the water can penetrate into the hollow space between it and the pressure hull itself. This ensures that the outer skin needed for surface travel is not damaged under water.

Surrounded by the clammy walls of the shelter, German shipyard workers are provided with little platforms from which to repair the boats that return severely damaged from a fighting mission.

According to the Office for Naval Construction, 12,750 workers were needed in the shipyards to do the repairs on 150 U-boats.

Since the staff was not entirely German but included many French shipbuilding specialists and since thousands of French workers were employed in the ports generally, it was easy for the enemy to keep abreast of how many boats at a time were confined to the floating pens and the docks and what were the departure and arrival dates. (About the boat itself there was nothing the English did not know: way back in 1940, the submarine U-30, its captain killed in action, was abandoned by its crew on the assumption that it would sink. The recovery of the vessel by a British commando unit remained a closely guarded secret until the end of the war.)

The extent to which the defeated French had to render tribute—officially known as "collaboration"—to the naval grandeur of their German captors emerges from an entry referring to a lecture organized by the Navy at the Headquarters of the Chiefs of Staff on February 4, 1944:

"Navy much more dependent than other two Forces on collaboration. On four bases alone (Brest, Cherbourg, Lorient, Toulon) collaborators number 93 French officers, approx. 3,000 enlisted men, 160 engineers, 680 technicians, and 25,000 workers. Tractors, floating cranes, steel net barriers, docks, power stations, and motor vehicles of all kinds are manned by these staff. Reinforcements and arms manufacture heavily, above-water ship repairs one hundred percent, dependent on French collaboration."

No wonder that whenever boats suffered damage that was not readily explicable and often mortally dangerous to the crew, the commanders would think of sabotage, curse the "chaos" in the shipyards, and alert their ranking superiors to their suspicions.

Two submarines in one of the floating docks of the St.-Nazaire shelter. To the right, a normal VII-C boat, to the left a "sea cow."

Taking on torpedoes is the worst; fourteen of these one-and-a-half-ton "eels" have to go into the tubes, into holders on the upper deck, and into bow and aft compartments. For this, the boat has to make fast at the pier where all the equipment is issued. This is the time for the "Torpedo Boys" to get going.

I am down in the bow. Here it looks like some underground workshop: loading rails along the ceiling, the gleaming chains of pulleys, walls lined with mattresses from berths that swing down at bedtime. The mind boggles at the thought that twenty-four men will soon move in and live here throughout the voyage. I have to take care not to bump my head.

The covers at the base of the torpedo tubes are unfastened and bluish-grayish daylight comes in through the loading hatch. "Slacken off!" I hear. "Let go! Let go, goddammit!"

The torpedo mechanic standing next to me shouts instructions: "Give us an eel." The bluish-gray moon of the hatch is reduced to an inverted crescent. Slowly, the eel comes gliding down the loading trough. There is no more light coming in now. A lot of shouting: "Slowly!"—"Hold it!"—"Get the stopper out of the way!"—"Easy does it!"—"I said slowly, goddammit to hell!"

Lying diagonally across the compartment, the torpedo looks even bigger than it is in fact. It is looped with bands of steel and maneuvered into a horizontal position along the loading rail. Its protective layer of grease reflects the sparse lights scattered about the room.

Now they are removing the protective bucket. The torpedo mechanic takes the warhead from a gray container and fits it to the torpedo. With skilled fingers he removes the seals. Then he reads off the number and takes it down in his notebook.

Five men reach up to grab hold of a horizontal set of pulleys and with as much heave-ho as in a tug-of-war they drag the primed torpedo into its tube.

This is what the early entries are like in a war log:

10/16. Boat leaves dock.
10/17. Fuel and lubricating oil taken on.
10/18. Run-through.
10/19. Trial run.
10/21. Radio drill, trimming practice, balancing the boat. Anti-aircraft ammunition, torpedoes, and dry goods taken on.
10/25. Perishable provisions taken on.

The responsibility for loading the torpedoes belongs to the First Watch Officers. From a special truck, a crane heaves up the torpedo, covered in grease, fitted with a protective bucket to shield its most vulnerable section, and then the "Torpedo Boys" maneuver it over the boat, suspended from a hook. It is lowered down a loading trough through the torpedo hatch into the bottom of the boat or stowed with the help of pulleys into the bow or stern compartments.

An entry in the war log of the Naval High Command dated October 10, 1941, contains the following comment on Germany's torpedo production:
". . . With a monthly completion rate of 1,450 torpedoes, the industry has increased reserves to a very satisfactory level. Experience has confirmed the Naval High Command's estimate of October 1940, that the average consumption of torpedoes would be 6.6 per month per boat. The aim now is to stockpile torpedoes in sufficient quantities to tide us over any extraordinary peaks of consumption or a higher rate of deployment as a result of some unavoidable change in offensive tactics, and we are already well on the way toward such a stockpile."
So there were plenty of torpedoes—but too few boats.

All supplies have to be passed down through a single narrow hatch. The bosun has to be everywhere, his watchful eye on everything. He reels off the catalogue for my benefit: "Fuel, water, lubricating oil, oxygen, alkali cartridges, spare ropes, oilskins—not to mention a million other bits and pieces. Most of the groceries are already on board." The navigator worries about everything, as usual. Ropes are the bosun's responsibility, provisions that of the second watch officer. I look pointedly at the piles on the pier and the chaos on deck. "Not far to go now," says the chief navigator, ignoring the fact that the entire deck aft is still littered with cardboard boxes, piles of large cans, nets full of sausages and sides of bacon, crates of apples and grapes. And more keeps coming all the time: cables, gumboots, escape apparatus, fur jackets, rubber garments. . . . Inconceivable that all of it will soon disappear into the belly of the boat before the order to "Cast off all lines and haul them in!" Up in the bow some parts of the gratings are still missing. Shipyard workers are crouched in the space below and struggling to fix them. There is a strong smell of oil fumes and burned paint. A tangle of cables emerges from the galley hatch, a large bale of cleaning twist is handed down, a bucket is heaved up. I hear someone say: "The freshwater tanks are leaking. They still have to be welded."

Since nobody knows exactly how long we will be away, the boat has to carry the maximum possible quantity of provisions. And since there is no proper space for storage, every nook and cranny must be filled up with groceries. The men squirreling the stuff away even find room for it under the ceilings of the narrow passageways. Anyone wanting to get through will simply have to keep his head down. Even in the control room, the very heart of the boat, crowded as it is with the steering equipment, machinery for operating periscopes, flood valves, drain pumps, and any number of other instruments and systems, sausages are dangling from the pipes overhead; it looks for all the world like the Hanging Gardens of Babylon.

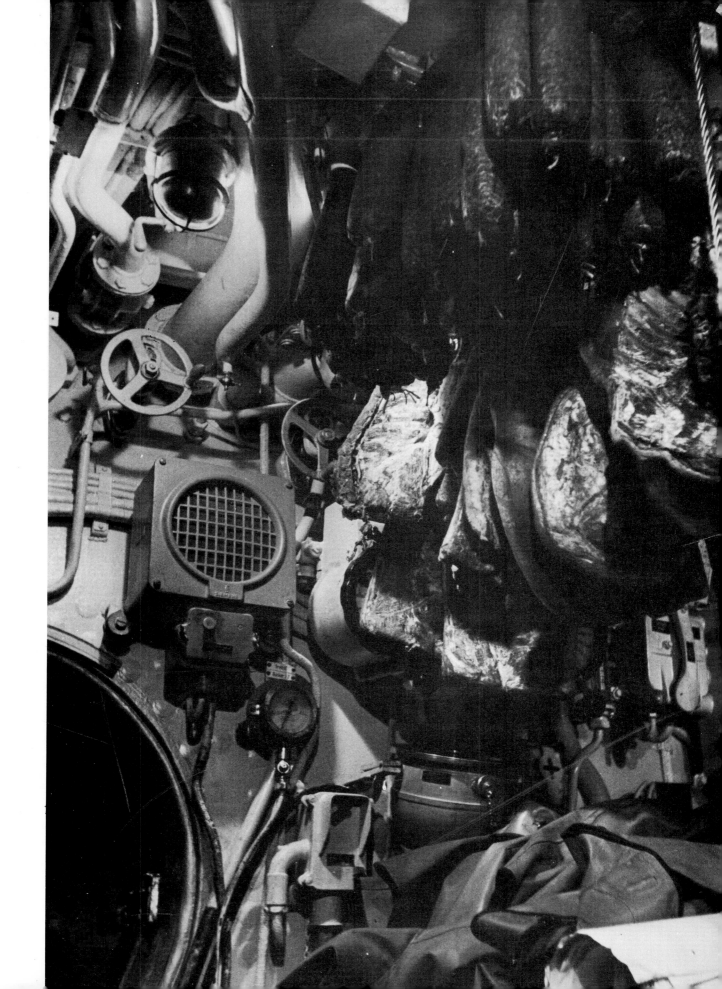

Departure—Toward the Theater of Operations

The skipper is wearing his most casual clothes: an ancient sweater and a gray leather jacket. He gives the orders for a roundabout course, the winding route that follows the shore. Pines yield to reddish-brown rocks, with the sea a dull gray beyond.

We exchange nothing but commonplaces, acting as though this is nothing more momentous than a trip to the railway station. "Lousy weather," says the commander, "bound to be foggy out there."

The upper deck has been cleared. Not a tool in sight, not a sack, not a crate. It's all spick-and-span. All cable ends are neatly coiled. Both the galley hatch and the torpedo supply hatch leading down to the bow compartment are shut tight. The boat is ready to get under way. The first watch officer orders the crew to stand to attention and walks over to the commander: "Permission to report: All hands present and accounted for. Engine room ready, upper and lower decks cleared for departure!"

"Thanks. Heil UA!"

The commander is a man of few words. Immediately he orders the men to their stations. The battery whistle bleats shrilly: once long, twice short.

The commander takes personal charge of the maneuver for departure. "Let go aft; haul in the sternline!" The cables splash into the water, are hauled in and coiled up. Several of the men are in high spirits, exchanging jokes with the dock workers. The military band starts up its instruments and all speech is drowned in a deafening tidal echo of sound. The last few flowers come fluttering down on the upper deck.

The signaler transmits a message to the blockade buster which will escort us through the minefields and afford us anti-aircraft cover.

While the engines are warming up, forward mooring cables are kept in place so that the boat will not bump against the side of the pier, and the fenders are withdrawn. "Hard a-port! Starboard engine ahead one third!"

The boat glides free of the pier. On the foredeck, four sailors are using boathooks to keep the bow in the clear. The mooring cables have fallen.

We emerge stern first from the cavernous bunker. The sudden flood of silvery light makes me close my eyes. Already, the lines are laid out on the upper deck again—for the maneuver which will take us through the lock.

It's high tide: we won't have to make fast again at the lock. "All hands on deck." Many of the stokers and mechanics take what will be their last look at daylight for the entire voyage.

Excerpts from the war log of U-96:

October 26

10:00. Cleared port. Put to sea. Northwest 2–3. Seas 1–2. C-2. Visibility good. Trimming trials.

21:48. Test dive. Submerged run. Torpedo exercises.

October 27

00:36. Passing U-boat. Identification signal. Responded with identification signal.

09:46. Practice alarm with emergency drill and deep dive. Hydroplane maneuvers and fire control practice.

10:55. Practice alarm.

15:44. Practice alarm.

16:03. Practice alarm. Weapons practice limited by weather conditions. Cruising in attack area.

October 28

Change of position 12 nautical miles.

The boat's theater of operations is in mid-Atlantic—a square designated by two numbers on a map. The navigator reckons that it will take the boat ten days at cruising speed to reach that particular square. We could get there more quickly if the commander ordered the diesels to be run at standard speed. But he has opted for cruising speed, in order to save fuel.

The helmsman up in the conning tower barely needs to bother: the line keeps marking one and the same number on the swinging compass: 265 degrees. The boat is moving steadily westward. Whenever possible, I am up on the bridge. The sight of our bow cutting through wave after wave makes me feel good inside. I screw up my eyes, curl back my lips. With bared teeth I bite the air. The spray tastes salty. We are carried by the ancient sea, lifted high and then released again. The human body must surrender to its motion.

For one last time the navigator makes use of his diopter to take a land bearing, which he immediately records on his route map of the voyage. From now on he will have to use astronomic instruments to get a fix on our boat's position.

Commander and Crew

Since we have been at sea, the commander has changed: formerly gruff and unforthcoming, now he is cheerful, even engaging, whenever he makes an appearance on the bridge. He usually has a fat cigar between the forefinger and middle finger of his right hand, puffs ostentatious clouds of smoke and otherwise makes it plain how glad he is to be back at sea. I am probably not the only one to be grateful for this attitude of his: having confidence in your commander is more important aboard a submarine than on any other vessel. After all, during a periscope attack, he is the only one who can actually see the enemy and who has to know exactly how far he might dare go.

The chief engineer is the commander's right hand. He is the absolute ruler of the engine rooms and responsible for precise depth control. He has to have something more than mere technical ability; as the man in charge of underwater steering he has to have a special sense which will enable him to anticipate the boat's every tendency to sink or to rise, because by the time these show up on the instruments, it is usually too late.

The first and second watch officers are in charge of their respective watches. They are naval officers and the commander relies on them whenever he is not himself on the bridge. Apart from this, number one is in charge of the torpedoes, while number two is responsible for the machine guns and the artillery.

Our crew is one of the most experienced. The engineers in charge of diesels and E-motors, the torpedo mechanics, the radio and hydrophone operators are all well trained, and so are the sailors.

Apart from the bosun, the navigator, the stokers, and several petty officers, they are all exceedingly young.

After the first few days, which were taken up with practice alarms, the commander withdraws from the regular activities on board. The curtains of his bunk are usually pulled shut. He sleeps with deliberation. His presence is felt rather than seen. His favorite maxim: "You must have all the sleep you can get, so that your nerves will be in good shape when it matters."

The lesson he keeps drumming into his watch officers: Don't try too hard to second-guess your adversary; he's set in his ways and will usually do the obvious thing. And don't pay too much attention to the whispers of your so-called intuition.

Years later, this is what the commander said: "As a submarine commander, you were ultimately on your own. Peering through the periscope, you made the decisions all on your own. During an attack, you were usually being chased by destroyers, threatened by depth charges, and at that moment you held the sole responsibility for the entire crew that was stuck with you inside that iron coffin. And so, every hit you scored was a kind of vindication of yourself to the crew."

Bridge Watch

Every watch is composed of one officer (the navigator in the case of the third watch), one petty officer, and two seamen. With their powerful binoculars, they incessantly scan the horizon and the air space above—each within his allotted sector of 90 degrees—for signs of danger or of prey, loners or convoys.

The war log of the Naval High Command has the following entry for December 8, 1940:

"The effectiveness of the submarine force rests entirely on its ability to put pressure on the enemy's major traffic and convoy routes. Poor weather conditions, long nights and short days limit the operational scope of the submarines and greatly diminish the chances of locating and holding on to the foe.

Hostile destroyers and observation planes force the U-boats to stay under water in daytime and deprive them of their own reconnaissance capability by reducing their field of vision to such a narrow area that it becomes extremely difficult, in many cases quite impossible, for them to operate successfully. Submarine combat forces will therefore need increasingly to be complemented directly by systematic air reconnaissance."

Such "systematic air reconnaissance" never emerged from the realm of wishful thinking. Certainly, some Condors would occasionally happen to catch sight of a solitary steamer or a convoy, but the position they transmitted was usually so much a product of guesswork that it was useless for finding the target.

Four straight hours of incessant vigilance—it can seem an eternity in any kind of bad weather. Every seagull will turn into an attacking aircraft, every scrap of cloud rising above the horizon will look like a trail of smoke, the contours of distant waves will seem outlines of ships.

Some threat to the boat may lurk on every side, come hurtling out of every cloud. Every crease in the grayish-green cloth of the sea may have a periscope hiding in it.

Cruising toward our theater of operations. Day in, day out, the same unchanging spectacle. Every day's run is like its predecessor.

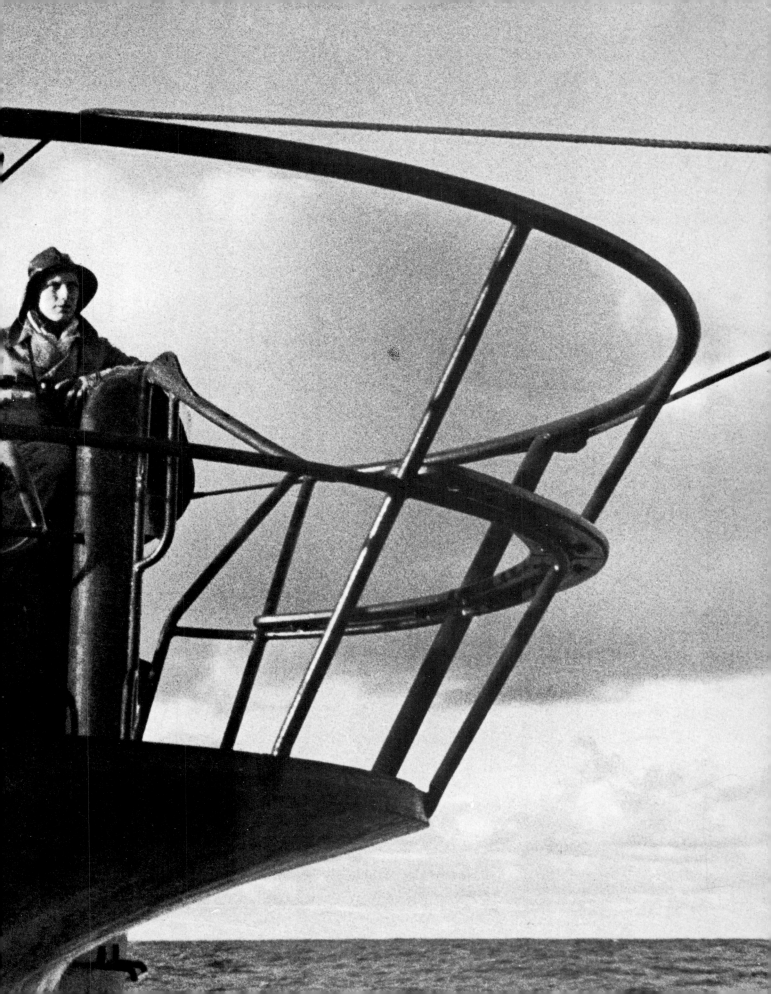

Test Dive

From the war log:

November 14
07:02 to 07:29. Test dive.
13:05. Dive to evade aircraft. Course to starboard 40 degrees.

November 16
01:18. Shadow to starboard at 120 degrees. Changed course toward it.
     Dropped suddenly out of sight at 01:40. Presumably a U-boat that has
     dived. Avoided the spot where it disappeared.
09:16–09:47. Dive to evade aircraft flying due north.

November 17
07:05–07:35. Test dive.

Daily test diving establishes the submarine's continued fitness for running
submerged. All vents and outboard plugs are checked, to see that they are
still watertight. There are a number of openings in the pressure hull to accommodate outboard cables and connecting rods—e.g., those for opening
and closing the torpedo doors. These are lined with flanges which are the
boat's many Achilles' heels.
Everything has to be carefully monitored at all times.
But the test dives also serve to balance the boat. That is to say, the boat's
equilibrium under water, which has been affected since the previous test dive
by the disposal of garbage, the consumption of water, or a change in the
surrounding sea's salt content, must be restored by taking seawater aboard.
Paradoxically, under certain conditions the tanks have to be blown for the
balance to be restored; namely, whenever a considerable amount of fuel has
been used up at high speed and replaced automatically by water. Given the
greater specific gravity of water as compared to fuel, all such changes have to
be duly noted—quite literally: the mate stationed in the control room actually

takes down every variation in the boat's weight in a special notebook. The chief hydroplane operator carefully prepares for every test dive by calculating what amounts of water have to be taken into the tanks or eliminated from them.

The ideal equilibrium is an unattainable state of perfect balance, with the weight of the boat (its total weight including all its contents) equal to the weight of the water it displaces.

The maneuver starts up with the bridge watch coming down: one petty officer and one seaman take up their positions at the hydroplanes, while the watch officer clamps down the hatch, fastening its heavy cover. Within seconds—as though there had been an alarm—the various rooms report that they are ready to dive. The order to stop diesels reaches the engine rooms by the method common to all ships: the optical signal is accompanied by the shrilling of a whistle. No one shouts an order in the engine rooms. Everything is transmitted by precise, much practiced hand signals. The fuel lever is switched to zero, so that the diesel oil no longer flows into the engines. Simultaneously, the big conduits leading to the outside—for the exhaust and for air intake—are shut off. As the diesel engines are unharnessed, the E-motors are put to work. They now transmit the energy stored in the batteries to the propeller shafts.

The "All clear to dive" is signaled to the control room.

The bow compartment does likewise, whereupon the chief engineer reports to the watch officer, "Ready to dive!"

The watch officer has already cranked the tower hatch home. Standing directly beneath the hatch, he shouts, "Flood!"

The chief repeats the order: "Flood!"

Now the sailors in the control room open the emergency evacuation vents and activate the flood valves: some of the evacuation vents have to be pulled and others turned. The air that gave the boat its buoyancy now escapes with a thundering roar from its tanks, making room for the seawater rushing in from below.

Without awaiting further orders, the hydroplane operators set the forward plane hard down and the after plane down. The boat dips and becomes noticeably bow-heavy; losing its buoyancy as the air escapes, the boat accelerates downward. The indicator on the depth gauge starts moving across the numbers on the dial. The tower is now below the water level. One final wave crashes against the bridge, and then all sounds of the sea are severed. There is sudden silence in the control room: no more vibration of diesels, no more humming of ventilators. Just a murmur of rushing water as the buoyancy cells are opened aft and the hissing of compressed air clearing the negative buoyancy tanks. Even the radio has lapsed into silence; no radio signal can reach us down here.

"Forward up ten, aft up fifteen!" the chief orders. The bow-heaviness is corrected. The current from the propellers aft strikes the upward-tilted hydroplane and slowly the boat grows stern-heavy. The boat is achieving its balance. Air bubbles that have clung to the corners of the buoyancy cells now escape. The chief reports to the commander, "Boat balanced!" Whereupon the commander orders, "Close vents!" If he now ordered the maneuver to be reversed, the air would remain in the ballast tanks.

In the process of its balancing, the boat has grown stern-heavy. This positions it correctly to attain the desired level dynamically from below with the help of the hydroplanes.

Without delay the commander orders, "Proceed to periscope depth." In accordance with the chief's instructions, the hydroplane operators press the appropriate buttons, and the indicator of the depth gauge retreats slowly, stopping at periscope depth. The watch officer takes up his periscope watch in the tower.

The commander calls for the speed to be reduced to dead slow. The chief calls for 25 gallons to be taken on and for 8 gallons to be trimmed forward. The boat still shows something of a tendency to rise, so the chief orders, "Both planes to neutral!" If everything is as it should be, the boat ought to be steady now, going neither up nor down. Like an airship it should proceed at an unchanging level. And indeed, the column of water inside the "Papenberg" is quite still.

During test dives the commander gives his orders to the helmsman in the conning tower, who passes them on.

The helmsman, who also operates the system of signals to the engine room, has no steering wheel to cope with. Only in dire emergency may he use the manual steering wheel which is located aft in the E-motor compartment. Here, in the conning tower and at the second steering position in the control room, the rudder is operated by buttons. Even when the boat is riding the surface, the helmsman sees nothing of the surrounding sea.

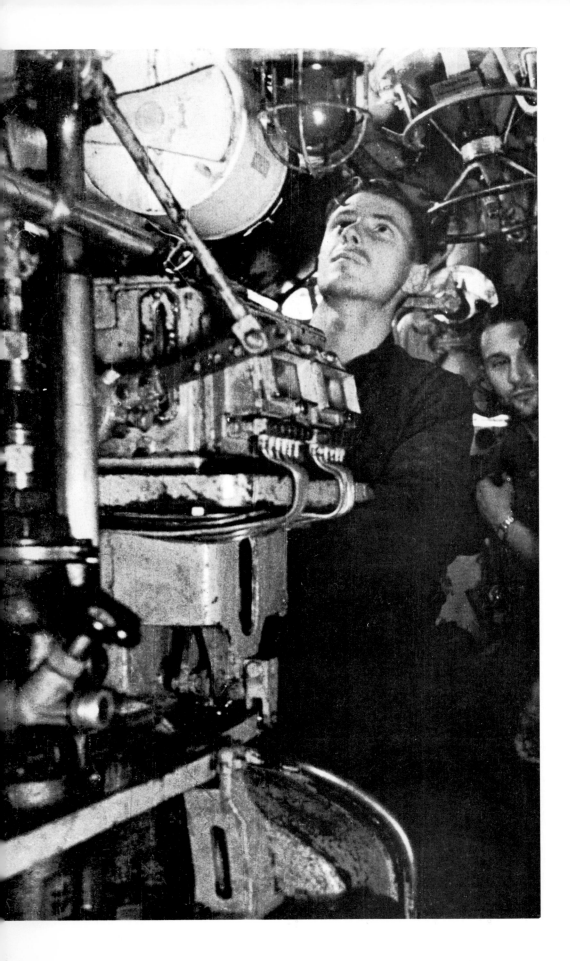

At the beginning of a test dive, the order to stop the diesels is transmitted to the engine room by means of the engine telegraph. Here, the diesel stoker keeps a close watch on the telegraph's indicator so as to react with lightning speed as he switches the fuel lever to zero. The E-motors are switched on the moment the diesel engines are turned off.

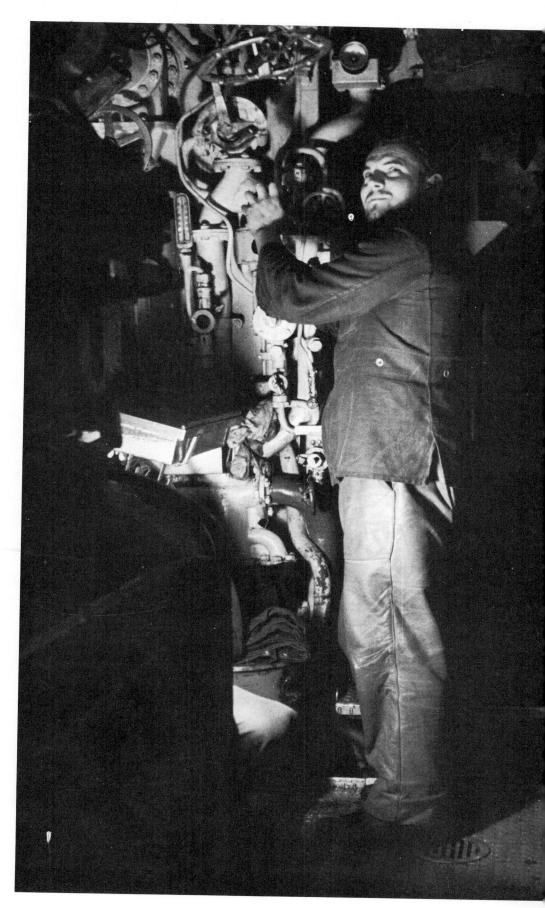

At the back of the starboard diesel, a diesel mate drains the exhaust valves. The draining mechanism lies between the inner and the outer exhaust valves. The water is discharged into the diesel bilge. The internal exhaust valves are activated by means of the hand wheels under the ceiling.

Satisfied, the chief nods his head. Now the boat can be maneuvered with minimal propeller action and easily maintained in a horizontal position by the hydroplanes fore and aft. A submerged submarine cannot be held at a given level unless its E-motors are on. The slightest change in weight, making the boat lighter or heavier than the water it displaces, will drive it up or down. Only the planes and the engines together can keep the boat dynamically at any given level.

The chief's voice cuts through the boat on the address system: "Ready to take soundings!" The sounding pipes are opened in the bow compartment and the engine room, and the sounding rods are smeared with chalk. The chief has his eyes glued to his instruments. When the boat is absolutely horizontal, he calls out: "Attention, zero!" Instantly, all the sounding rods are pushed down as far as they will go, withdrawn and read off. The messages come in one by one from the different rooms:

"Torpedo Cell Number 1—125 gallons."

The control room mate closes the air valve of the diesel engines on the ceiling of the control room—this is a valve in the conning tower wall which lets air into the engines.
Right: As soon as the men are ordered "To diving stations," two members of the bridge watch take up their positions at the hydroplanes. The hydroplanes are operated by pressing down the corresponding buttons with the palm of the hand.

"Torpedo Cell Number 2—160 gallons."
The control room mate jots down every message in the diving log book. The figures he has calculated are supposed to match those actually announced as closely as possible.

Only now does the commander put in an appearance in the control room, climbing in through the circular hatch. "Everything okay?"
"All in order, Herr Kaleunt!"
"What was the trimming differential?"
"Twenty-five gallons too light and eight stern-heavy."
"Was that worked out by the control room mate?"
"Yessir."
"To the control room mate—not too bad!"
We all know that such praise from the commander means top marks. The control room mate should be pleased.
The commander orders another deep dive, just in case.

The E-motor mate switches the starboard E-motor to the requisite speed.

Right: The bridge watch has come down into the boat, with the watch officer coming in last to shut the hatch behind him. Beneath the address system which transmits orders, the helmsman stays put in the tower.
The hermetic tower hatch is a symbol of the claustrophobia aboard the submarine.

The pressure under water puts a tremendous strain on our steel cylinder. Total silence reigns inside the boat. All those standing in the control room keep an anxious eye on the depth-gauge needle. Only the chief moves about, checking that all the plugs are secure. Then he orders the drain pumps into action. Draining? At this point? I close my eyes, trying to concentrate: the boat is being compressed, displacing less water, getting heavier—*ergo:* drain pumps.

The whole boat starts to creak and crack. Eventually the noise is so loud it sounds like someone banging against the steel. The depth needle is still pushing slowly on. It would seem that the commander means to go to the ultimate limit. But what exactly is the ultimate limit here? No one knows for certain how deep the boat can go. The figure quoted by the shipyard is a joke. Which means, in case of doubt, when the boat is being bombarded with depth charges it simply has to go farther and farther down, beyond the level at which depth charges explode.

The chief stands behind the two hydroplane operators to supervise the trim. The dials show that the front hydroplane is at neutral, the one astern at 5 degrees down. During a trial dive the boat is aimed at an approximate level of sixty feet. Normally there is no periscope observation.

The only member of the crew who still has contact with the outside world is the sound man.

The control room mate operating the flooding and draining pumps. In keeping with the orders transmitted to him by the man in charge of the trim, he opens or closes the valves of the stabilizing tanks. The test dive will show whether prior calculations correspond to reality. The balance of the boat must also be adjusted. This is achieved by means of the trim cells at both extremes of the boat, which are roughly equivalent to the balancing pole of a tightrope walker—though here the "pole" works lengthwise.

Whenever there are diving tests, the chief is in his element. His trickiest responsibility is the trimming operation, and he has to control it perfectly. Totally geared to his commander, he has to think along the same lines, be on the same wave-length, and grasp intuitively how any action within the boat will affect the trim. When it really counts, there is no time for asking questions or for having another go. When the commander is running a periscope attack, the chief has to counter every one of the boat's upward or downward impulses in good time, in order to make sure that the periscope will neither emerge so far as to be visible to the enemy, nor be engulfed to the point where the commander can no longer see.

The chief himself cannot see what goes on up above. And yet he has to react without delay; for example, he has to flood the very instant a torpedo goes off in order to make good the weight loss—and he even has to anticipate a salvo, because so much sudden buoyancy cannot be checked an instant after the firing: it would force the boat to the surface.

The diesel engines are still. The hatches of the engine room are closed. To the left of the picture, a flattened funnel and leading into it the pipes through which the fuel comes in from the storage tanks. This funnel serves to channel diesel oil, water, and waste into a refuse tank lying beneath the floor plates. On the ceiling, the hand wheels for the internal exhaust valves; in the center a loudspeaker linked to the address system and to the radio; to the right, the lever of the lubricating pump.

The diesel mate at the starboard engine. He makes use of the time the diesels are out of action to test the temperature of the rocker bearings by feeling them.

When it comes to surfacing, advantage is taken of natural dynamics. In order to increase the pressure on the hydroplanes, the E-motors are switched to high speed. At low and medium speed, the batteries are switched to run together.

In the engine room, the reserve fuel pump is the first turned on; it feeds fuel into the engine systems. Even before the diesels are in motion, the indicator taps are opened and compressed air pushes the fuel through, in order to establish that no water has got into the cylinders and also to eliminate particles of soot through the indicator valves. (Whenever the pressure diminishes, the piston rods are in danger of breaking.) The message "The diesels are ready" is relayed from the engine room to the control room by word of mouth.

In the control room, the main air pressure valve on the compressed air distributor—that vertical agglomeration of multiple valves and multiple hand wheels which we call "the Christmas tree"—is opened to free the passage of air to buoyancy cells 1, 3, and 5. Once the boat has regained sufficient buoyancy so that the conning tower hatch is above water, the main air pressure valve is turned off again.

Now the pressure is equalized by opening the top and tail valves of the engine. This allows the escape of the excess pressure which builds up inside the

The E-motor mechanic stops the electric motors as soon as we surface. In the engine room (right), the diesel stoker has pumped lubricating oil through the mechanism to grease it thoroughly and set the fuel lever, which is next to the starting lever, at the desired level. Now he presses the starting lever downward, and air rushes into the cylinder. In a moment the boat will once again be running on diesel engines like an ordinary surface vessel.

boat whenever the trimming tanks are ventilated inward, and makes it possible for the conning tower hatch to be opened "normally." If the pressure were not equalized, then the tower hatch would pop like a champagne cork and be torn from the watch officer's grasp.

The bridge watch has been standing by. As soon as the watch officer opens the hatch, its members move to take up their positions.

When it comes to expelling the last quantities of water from the buoyancy cells—in this case from cells 1, 3, and 5—these are blown out with the oily diesel exhaust gases, partly because that helps prevent corrosion, but mainly in order to save the compressed air in the air banks.

We can hear the sound of the diesel engines starting up. The chief is watching the needle on the air pressure gauge. When it indicates the proper pressure, he starts opening the valves on the conduits through which the diesel exhaust fumes make their way to the buoyancy cells. Then he reports to the bridge: "Both sides of three blown out!" There is a loud hiss every time the chief opens a valve. When all the cells are blown, the commander orders: "Dismiss from diving stations!"

Radio Operation

However complete a commander's independence when it comes to tactical decisions, his boat is nonetheless guided across the oceans by the leash that is its radio. For that is the only way to fight a convoy battle.

From the war log of the Naval High Command, July 22, 1941:

"In response to our enquiry regarding the present state of the submarine war, U-Boat Headquarters has issued the following opinion, which is categorically endorsed by the Naval High Command:
"1. The main problem of the submarine war is still that of locating the foe when traveling in convoy.
"2. The attempt to control a concentration of sea routes further to the west has not been successful. Fog and adverse weather conditions have been mainly responsible."

The radio shack is right next to the control room, opposite the captain's "cabin." When the boat is submerged, the radioman can still receive long waves down to a depth of some sixty to seventy feet; that is, when the radio aerial is about thirty feet under water. But short and medium waves cannot penetrate the sea.

The boat receives a radio signal. I suddenly realize that we are not following our course out here all on our own. On huge maps in the Commander in Chief's headquarters, little flags indicate the positions of the various boats. Now and again the boats emit short signals saying where they are, and the little flags are moved accordingly. As soon as any boat gives notice by radio that it has sighted the foe, other boats in the vicinity are directed to the scene by radio.
I tensely await the deciphered text of the message. As it happens, it does not concern us at all. Another boat has been ordered to shift its position seventy miles westward. Apparently a convoy is expected to pass through at that point. I ask the navigator to show me the exact spot on the chart. It is close to the U.S. coastline; i.e., many days' sailing from where we are.
A little later we pick up a radio message meant for a boat that is close to Iceland and one for another that is operating in the area of Gibraltar. Suddenly the oceans are no longer empty. VII-C's are everywhere, looking for convoys.
All messages, not just the ones addressed to us, are picked up and recorded by our radioman in the war log:

05:00. From U-Boat Headquarters: L occupy T's previous attack area.

05:30. From R: hydrophone bearing. Convoy on Square XY leading westward.

07:10. Enemy convoy in sight. Square XW. 160 degrees. 10 sea miles. U-430.

08:22. Foe running zigzag course around 50 degrees. Speed 9 sea miles. U-520.

15:30. Convoy traveling in several columns. Heavily protected on all sides. Speed 9 sea miles. Course 100 degrees. U-430.

Well beyond our reach. During the night we pick up messages which report success: Convoy square XW westerly course. Nine sea miles. West wind 7. Rain. Three steamers of the escort hit, though one not actually seen sinking. Depth charges. U-82.

Very heavy seas. Low temperatures. Steamer D of convoy sunk. U-430.

The radioman is wearing his listening gear with only one of the earpieces over his ear. In this way he can hear both incoming Morse signals and, through the ear that is free, orders from inside the boat.

Staff Headquarters has given the strip of operations we patrol the high-sounding name Störtebecker. No doubt a convoy is predicted in the area. We are just one prong in the rake which is expected to furrow a huge expanse of ocean.

This may sound plausible, but experience proved otherwise. To get some idea of the actual dimensions of the problem, to understand the relation of the width of the rake to the size of the surface to be raked, one must imagine pulling such a rake at right angles, usually, to the supposed course of a convoy—as in some kind of regular pattern across the sands of a vast beach.

It is difficult to settle on the width of such a strip allotted to a "submarine rake" of, let's say, ten boats in the Atlantic, because so many factors determine each individual boat's field of vision, which in turn determines the distance between the boats. Assuming that the weather is good and given that the highest tip of a steamer's mast will rise some 130 feet above sea level, it can be reckoned that the external signs of enemy shipping will be visible over a distance of twelve to fifteen miles. This would mean that the distance between boats should not exceed twenty-four to thirty miles, if the dragnet is to be effective.

But, in fact, the boats were deployed more loosely, because High Command, subtle as ever, reckoned that no convoy was likely to turn up precisely halfway between two boats. In good weather, they were therefore prepared to risk a distance of up to fifty miles or more between two boats—but how often is the weather good in mid-Atlantic, and along with it the visibility? At best, during the summer, visibility is ten to twenty sea miles. But in winter it contracts to way less than a ten-mile radius, and then the advance patrols assigned to the boats were a dragnet full of holes, or else the "rake" was far too narrow.

To make a comparison: The radar range of an aircraft flying at a height of around six thousand feet measures thirty sea miles at least—*whatever* the weather. And even when the weather is bad, an aircraft can "see" much more than a whole chain of submarines, because it has the speed to allow it to patrol its beat in a very short time.

The main problem for the Allies was to locate the submarine patrols in good time, and thus avoid them. For the Germans, there was never a hope of battle without a search first; the Allies always had a chance to spot and avoid the German submarines before having to defend themselves against them.

The chief unfolds a map of Germany on the mess table: "Move over for a minute!"
It is a large map—all brown and green.

As though by previous arrangement, all three of us immediately start scrutinizing different bits of it. I myself am looking for the Starnberger See. It has seemed very far away in recent weeks, and I have rarely spared a thought for the countryside around the lake. But now there is this map lying on the mess table. None of us says a word. Each is enhancing the green or brown spaces with memories of his own.

The navigator is busying himself on the chart chest, and I ask him: "Well, what kind of weather are we going to get, then?"

He raises the dividers, turns toward me, and gives a detailed answer, which is quite unlike him: "Cyclones, colliding fronts, cold front predominating . . . all kinds of crap, but in the end there'll be no real change. No real improvement, though the barometer looks good!"

"Since when does the weather take no notice of the barometer?" I say, trying to tease him.

The navigator turns his eyeballs heavenward. He's not prepared to take on such extreme meteorological innocence. Shrugging his shoulders, he goes back to work with triangle and dividers.

Every day it's the same old drag: a weary, stultifying crawl along a beat laid down by High Command. The course run by our boat on the chart looks like the doodling of an imbecile.

I spare a cynical thought for those who've joined the Navy to See the World. And what do they see? They see switchboards, hand wheels, cables, instruments. Instead of foreign shores, this mindless chugging up and down.

Just for a change, I have myself assigned to a watch as helmsman. The boat has a dirty habit of swerving sideways—sometimes fore and sometimes aft. In an effort to correct this, I overdo the compensation and push the rudder too hard in the other direction: the number of degrees I was aiming for on the dial slips by the steering pointer, I want to hold it back but cannot, the boat veers to the opposite side. It's terrible when you can't see the bow. Right in front of my nose there's no view of the open sea, just a wall tinted white, full of pipes and levers: blind man's buff.

"Look at our wake. Isn't it pretty?" I hear someone scoff up above. There is another rudder indicator up on the bridge, where the first watch officer, who happens to be on duty just now, can always keep an eye on what the helmsman is doing.

I struggle to stop the disk in front of me. I glower at it as though my stare were enough to bring it to a halt—an insane exercise, just like those puzzles where you have to maneuver tiny little balls or mice into particular holes. At one point I even drum my fingers on the glass: "Come on, you lousy bastard—just behave yourself!"

From below, the mocking voice of the chief: "Oh, I see, it's our new helmsman! I was wondering what had got into our tugboat."

Leaning on both elbows and with his feet well back so that the inclination of his body will give him a firmer hold on the chart table, the commander is studying the open map. He cradles his head in his palms and stares at the grid of squares.

"They seem to have taken to going in a wide northerly curve. This is where we should be right now." Holding the dividers horizontally he sketches out an area which is no different from where we are except for different numbers. The commander is gazing so intensely at the plain blue surface with its finely drawn squares that he seems to be expecting the mere act of contemplation to produce a revelation. Eventually he heaves a sigh, shakes his head with exasperation, waves his arms about haphazardly, and starts cursing: "This goddam frigging around—fuck the whole thing!"

"The Eyes of the Boat," the bridge guards of the watch, must never ever tire. They are bound to total vigilance—even after weeks of frigging around.

I scramble up on deck. The gray grizzled sea, the dreary gray sky, the just-a-little-bit-lighter blob of putty which is supposed to be the sun, but looks more like the eyeball of a dead calf—none of it is a particularly happy sight. And there is no real dramatic darkness, no really dismal gloom—just an in-between grayness that is actually nauseating.

"Morose" might be the word to describe what the sky is like. Morose—not bad. "Gross" has the same drawn-out sound to it. Gross tonnage, gross error, gross, morose—suddenly it all gets your goat.

The days trudge by in a regular rhythm of watches and dog watches. The "dog watchers" eat or sleep as best they can, given the bustle all around them.

The cook is a man sorely tried. All the traffic to the diesels and the E-motors has to go through his galley, and the ladder leading up to the galley hatch curtails what little room he has left to turn around in. To provide fifty grown men with all their meals in all weather and with only two hot plates to work on is no picnic. And even at night those on bridge duty still clamor for hot coffee, alias "the night watchman."

The job of steward, of waiting at table as it were, is hardly popular. In the bow compartment and in the crew's quarters it's someone else's turn every day. Mates, petty officers, and officers are served by one and the same steward throughout the voyage. On submarines the stewards of officers and petty officers have to clamber their way, laden with dishes, jugs, and platters all filled to the brim, through the narrow circles of two pressure-proof bulkheads—"Like circus lions through a hoop," mocked those who were spared the drudgery.

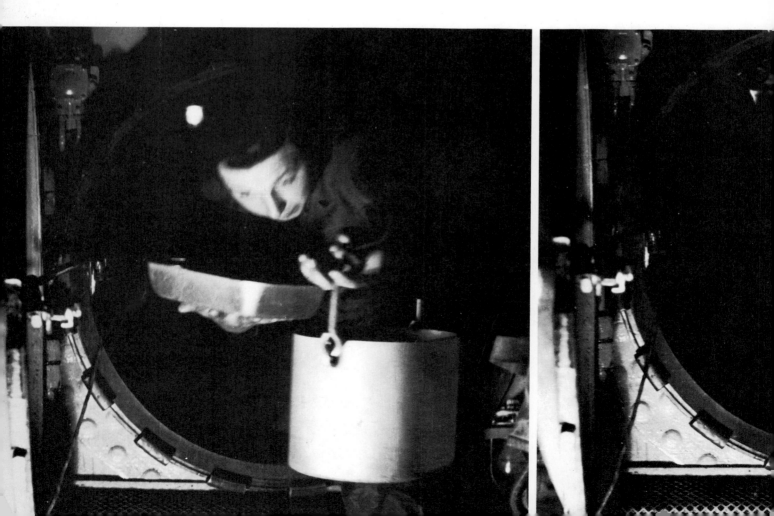

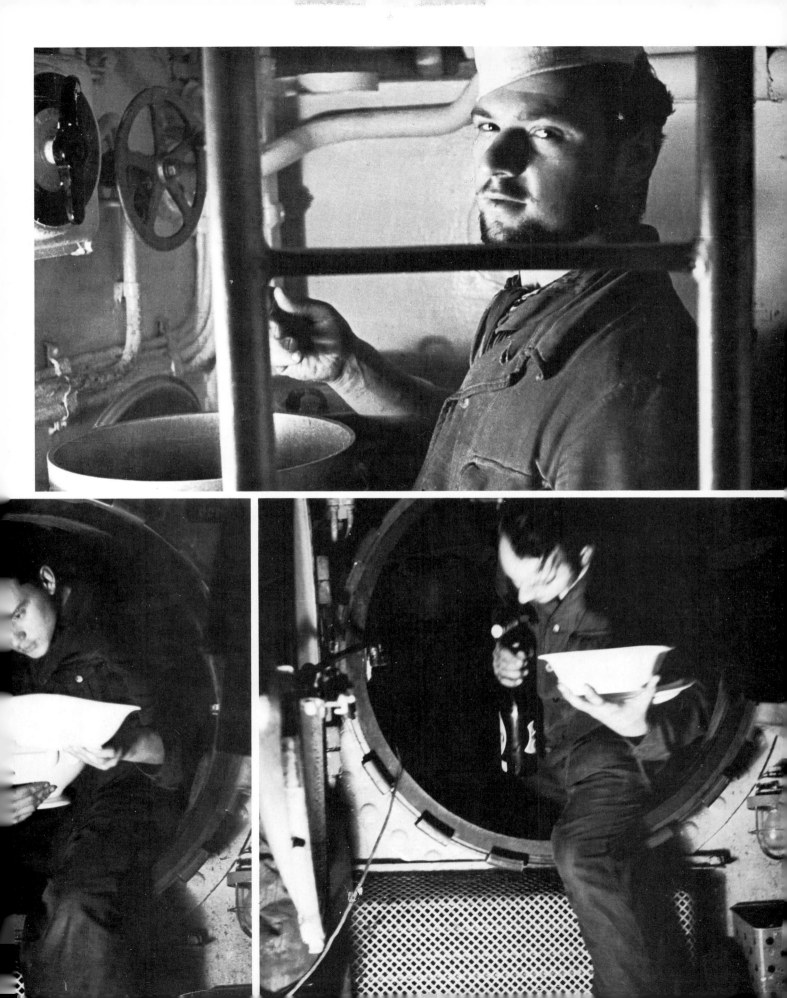

Left: Bow compartment with the bunks to starboard aft and the folding table with its leaves down. Standing by the open bulkhead, our cook.

Right: View of the bow compartment. The greater part of the crew sleeps, eats, and lives in this cave measuring no more than a few cubic feet. On both sides, collapsible bunks and, swinging from the ceiling, hammocks where the men of the dog watch are asleep.

At every change of watch, always the selfsame sight: heavy seas, and our bow charging into the green breakers with their white crests. As the bow pierces the surge, rears up, shakes off its load and bears down into the next formidable wave, it is the very symbol of strength and tenacity, holding its own against the elements.

Torpedo Inspection

One of the regular jobs aboard is that of inspecting the torpedoes, which must be pulled from their tubes and tested, "regulated."

Every four or five days, the bow compartment is transformed into a machine shop. Hoist rings are fixed to the carriage on the loading track and the floor breach of the torpedo tube is opened. The torpedo, thickly coated with grease, is extracted from its tube with the aid of a horizontal hawser and strung to the loading carriage. If the torpedo uses compressed air for propulsion the air tanks are refilled. The motor is checked to make certain that all its bearings and axles are functioning smoothly. Rudder and hydroplane controls are tested and the lubrication points filled with oil.

It may sound pretty simple, but in the crowded confines of the bow compartment it is very hard work.

Since there should always be three torpedoes in readiness, only one is inspected at a time.

During the first phase of the war, the most common torpedoes were the G7A's, running on compressed air. Later on, they were largely replaced by G7E torpedoes driven by E-motors, which did away with the earlier model's revealing trail of bubbles. These torpedoes had a diameter of just over twenty inches and carried a load of approximately eight hundred pounds of high explosives. All in all, they weighed some three thousand pounds. Each one cost about 40,000 Reichsmarks to make (though such calculations of cost are probably meaningless when industry is on a war footing).

The torpedoes varied significantly with regard to their detonators. They were either conceived for concussion detonation or for magnetic detonation, activated by the target's magnetic field, while some were capable of both. These "backbreakers" exploded directly *beneath* the target vessel. The famous "Zaunkönig" model was an "acoustic" torpedo. Launched in the general direction of the enemy, it would home in on its target by making straight for the loudest noise in the vicinity. The ultimate refinement consisted of surface-scanning torpedoes, which were not aimed at a specific target, but directed at the whole herd of steamers in convoy; these torpedoes would follow a zigzag course through the convoy until eventually they either hit a vessel or simply foundered, having exhausted their reserves of energy.

The routine ticks on, as regular as clockwork. Four-hour watches for the seamen, six-hour watches in the engine rooms. The fuel reserves diminish, the filth accumulates, and our beards grow longer.

The word "hygiene" is greeted by U-boat crews like a comedy routine. Fresh water is precious—to be saved for brushing one's teeth and an occasional mouthwash. Anyone determined to have a proper bath—for which there is no

This is what the bow room looks like when the reserve torpedoes are still under the floor boards. There's not even enough room to stand up straight because of the hammocks swinging under the ceiling. Here, up front, the rolling is worse than anywhere else in the boat. The torpedo mate has seniority in the bow compartment; he is the only petty officer who sleeps here—right next to his place of work, since the bow compartment is where the torpedoes are.

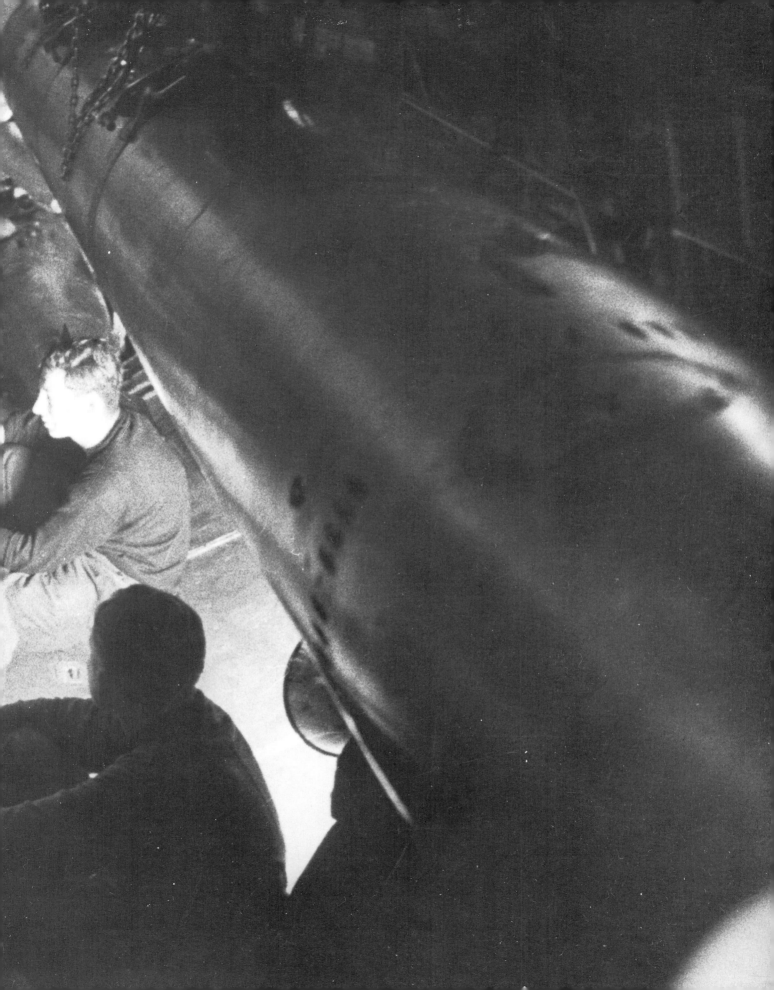

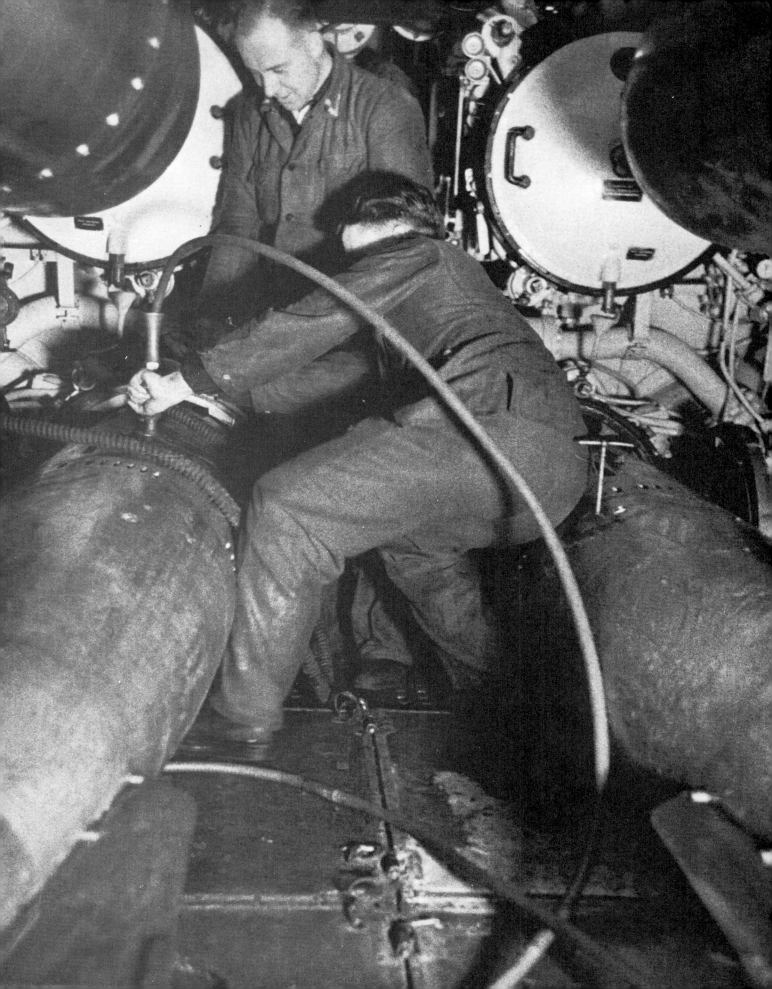

room in a submarine, and which is quite impossible when the seas are high—has to use saltwater softened with a special soap. Hardly anyone even thinks of shaving. Beards are tended with loving care; when the sub comes back to port their thickness will make the reception committee on the pier realize just how long the voyage has been. No matter how long the period at sea, no one is encouraged to change his underwear. The men have a preference for what they call "whore's undies," which are black, on the grounds that "they don't get so dirty."

The entry in my diary says Thursday. Another new tack. Seas so high that no weapons practice is possible. The weather seems to be favoring the enemy, of whom there's not a trace to be seen.
Friday: radio silence, apart from enemy reports. Apparently there are now a number of boats in our area.
No sign, however, of the expected convoy. It looks as though we are fishing in a pond that has no fish in it at all. A light wind from the northwest. Stratocumulus clouds up high, but layers of haze close to the water. The goddam haze robs us of what little visibility we have. It shrinks our basin-size horizon to a thimble-size one. It would have to be a stroke of the most freakish good luck for a ship to drift across our tubes in godawful conditions like these.

Our radio picks up the following message: "Search quadrant XY. Reconnaissance plane in distress at sea."
We are all rather baffled. We had no idea that we still had any sea reconnaissance planes left. But in a matter of seconds the Old Man is at the chart table. And in no time he's begun to give rudder and engine orders.
I can see it all in my mind's eye: poor devils, drifting somewhere in the sauce. How long can a plane hold out above water? God knows whether the fix on their position is really accurate.
We charge full speed ahead toward the spot where they're supposed to be. The Old Man keeps asking what time it is. He's glued to the bridge. Now he's asking for the signal gun. I hand it up to him. Then I scramble topside myself.
I am appalled to see how high the waves are. In seas like these the airmen cannot last long.
The Old Man raises his arm and pulls the trigger. The cartridge bursts out hissing. A white light unfurls above our heads. We stare as though mesmerized into the floodlit water.

Later on, when the search has been abandoned, depression sets in. Random talk about the dubious reliability of the machines in which we have to place our trust. The second watch officer says that he finds them frightening and thinks of them as *creatures,* treacherous and oppressive.

I am stuck with a nickname: Lieutenant Leatherrag, because whenever I'm up on the bridge I keep asking every few minutes for a dry leather rag to polish my camera lenses.
In the midst of a storm I finally give up. Instead of smearing salt all over the lens, I just lick it with my tongue.

*"Good visibility is half
the battle!" is the motto
of submarine crews.*

The sunny sector is the bugbear of those on bridge watch:
enemy aircraft attack straight out of the sun.

"Old salt!" mocks the commander when he sees what I'm doing.

One never knows: did the shutter jam this time or didn't it? Have the delicate innards of the camera survived that last shower of seawater? Will anything at all show up on the film?

One of our fellow submarines has signaled that it can no longer dive. Now it is merely an exceedingly vulnerable surface vessel, exposed to enemy discovery and attack, and practically defenseless. Not even someone lost in a desert could feel more abandoned than every man-jack on that boat deprived of its ability to dive. Probably it is just a matter of a leaking outboard valve—a mere nothing in so finely articulated a mechanism—but even such trivial damage is sufficient to rob a boat of its most precious asset, the protection of under-water invisibility.

Four of us are sitting crouched together in the officer's mess. Nothing to report, is what the commander writes in his war log. A few bare figures which tell the uninitiated nothing at all, and one or two totally meaningless sentences. Taciturnity is the order of the day.

Suddenly the Old Man puts his pen aside and says, to himself rather than to us: "This is probably not the way most people imagine the submarine war—or us, for that matter! They probably never think of it as working for a haulage contractor."

That strikes me as very close to the bone: a haulage contractor. We haul torpedoes, artillery shells, machine-gun ammunition—we haul the whole lot mindlessly back and forth, because we can't get hold of the right addressee.

Bullshit! I tell myself by way of an interruption. Better to ask the commander how many other boats he thinks there are crisscrossing the Atlantic right now like us.

The commander doesn't know either.

"The bunkers were pretty full up when we left," he murmurs finally. "Some boats are on their way to us, others on their way back or patrolling areas a long way from here. That leaves just a handful for these parts—perhaps about twenty."

And these twenty boats are expected to form a dragnet that can catch a convoy? It's a net with hundred-mile mesh. On a map, our range of vision is one single pinprick. So there's a pinprick right here and miles and miles away there's another one. There's enough room between the two for whole convoys to proceed unnoticed in stately progress—in ordered phalanx if they so chose. This kind of naval warfare is far too much a matter of chance.

Everybody has stopped talking. I have time to think about it all: this same scene around me multiplied twenty times over—with minor modifications for the larger boats operating farther south. There the men are less crowded and can sit about half-naked in the heat. Around Murmansk, meanwhile, the men on bridge watch are wearing furs. We really are a worldwide shipping firm, roaming from Murmansk to Cape Town to the territory of the Japs.

I fritter the time away. I toss and turn, I try and rest my head on my left arm, but I can't find a comfortable position. I try out my small pillow between my cheek and my arm—that's better.

At one point I wake up because the engine noise has stopped. The room is dimly lit by a single light bulb. Suddenly I can hear the waves beating against the sides of the boat.

The alarm sounds in the middle of the night. Ragged snatches of thought race indistinctly through my brain like underexposed film.
Below me, everything is one vast grumbling cursing surge toward the hatch. A voice rings out from the loudspeakers: "Belay alarm! Belay alarm!" And then, from the control room: "That was our friend Mr. Rott, our good friend Seaman Rott!"
The second watch officer is exasperated enough to be forthcoming: "I put the fellow up in the tower as helmsman. The idiot hit the alarm bell by mistake!"
Seaman Rott can thank his lucky stars that he's sitting topside in the tower. You could find one or two who'd gladly take him apart.

I still have some residual sense of passing time. So do the others, apparently. A washbasin with water has been set up in the control room. One by one, they strip to the waist and wash, then they part their hair meticulously in front of a dull looking-glass hanging underneath the gyro-compass. It must be Sunday.

Just like the paramilitary work battalions: the ablution never went beyond the waistline there either. No drop of water ever reached those parts which were most in need.

The cook has produced seven large Madeira cakes; he wants me to take a photograph of them.

"I can hardly move an inch in the galley. There's no way I can stand back far enough. But the moment they're out on the mess table, I promise I'll take a picture!"

At lunchtime we get strawberries and cream for dessert. "Coffee and cake" is scheduled for 15:30. That's when I'll do it, just to keep the cook happy.

"If only we'd unloaded the eels!" I hear one of the seamen moan. The wish is all the more heartfelt in view of the coffee party to come. There's still no room to set up a mess table in the bow compartment. Up front you can only sit cross-legged, since the reserve torpedoes occupy the center passage beneath the floor boards: resting on wooden blocks, they cut another couple of feet off the headroom in the bow compartment, which is already as low as a gallery in a mineshaft on account of the hammocks suspended from the ceiling. Here in the bow, it is not uncommon for the men actually to look forward to enemy action: at least it clears a space.

The chief engineer has shaved his cheeks but left a goatee. He looks the spitting image of Conrad Veidt as Rasputin.

The first watch officer has to eat after everyone else, because he's on bridge duty. We sit there ostentatiously glued to his every move, which makes him quite jittery—a fair exchange because he tends to give us the jitters with his table manners. At breakfast he picks even the tiniest black specks from his porridge with a great display of distaste. We have to watch him at it all too often.

The chief tells me to keep my knees to myself. His bitch is that if I keep pressing my knees against the lowered guard rail of the table, I'll soon force it off its hinges. The chief is not just obsessed about his diesels: he worries about every nut and bolt on board.

The second watch officer can't laugh any more. One of his cheeks is swollen. "What darling round cheeks you have," mocks the chief.

The second watch officer is afraid he may get worse—there isn't a doctor aboard. Time and time again he fiddles about with a flashlight in front of his shaving mirror. But he can't quite manage to coordinate the mirror, the light and the inside of his mouth.

The chief takes malicious pleasure in describing what horrors may await him:". . . if nothing else will do the trick, we can always fix a drill to the E-motor."

What a tedious day. At daybreak I already had a hunch that it was going to be a dead loss.

We've been assigned to patrol yet another new outpost. For all we know, the gentlemen of the Staff are throwing dice to decide which square on the map they want us to search next.

A radio report informs us that German submarines have sunk an aircraft carrier in the Mediterranean. Wonder why the report says U-boats? At any rate, there's nothing doing in *these* parts.

The commander comes shinning up the ladder, surveys water and sky with skepticism, and gives vent to his temper: nothing in sight. We seem to be looking for the proverbial needle in a haystack.

"Rien ne va plus," grumbles the commander. "Not a soul anywhere." The entire ocean seems devoid of ships.

He volunteers an explanation: "They're no fools. Sometimes they'll opt for a course close to Greenland, and sometimes they head all the way south—as far down as Gibraltar. We've got nothing on our side but sheer luck. It would be lousy if they had a fix on our movements."

Periscope Attack

We are right in the middle of lunch. The second watch officer appears and reports to the commander, who has just finished what was on his plate: "Watch officer relieved—nothing out of the ordinary."

The second watch officer is pulling off his rubber pants when there's a report from the bridge: "To the commander: masthead off the port bow!"

The commander starts from the leather sofa like an uncoiling spring and rushes aft past the second watch officer, who is staggering about, still struggling with his pants.

The chief is likewise on his feet and pushes his way between my back and the wall of lockers.

The convoy we've been looking for all these weeks! Or is it—immediately, my heart sinks—a destroyer? Masthead—that sounds bad!

The visibility is atrocious. I have trouble making out what we've apparently sighted.

"Doesn't look like a destroyer," growls the commander.

"Must be an unaccompanied steamer—peculiar!"

The commander calls for the navigator. The navigator is on the spot at once, as though by magic.

"Take this down for the war log: 'Unaccompanied vessel sighted at nine nautical miles. Visibility moderate to poor.' "

The commander raises his binoculars again. Now he's growling through his hands, cupped around them: " . . . suppose we should say something about the speed . . . I'd guess a good ten sea miles. But let's run alongside for a while first. It could well be more."

Our wake has changed—it has unfurled like the wings of a bird aroused from sleep.

The engine noise too has taken on a different sound: it's now a steady roar. The diesels are going full out: the chase is on.

I leave the bridge to go and fetch my camera.

In the U-room an off-duty diesel mate has a question: "A misfortune, with four letters?" He looks up at me expectantly. I stare back at him as though confronted with a lunatic. Crossword puzzles? At a time like this? At once I recover my self-control. Mustn't lose face! A four-letter word for misfortune? I have to close my eyes in order to think clearly: *ruin*—that might be it.

"Ruin," I say casually.

The diesel mate is taken aback. "What?"

"Ruin. Like urine—just swap the first two letters and knock off the 'e.' "

"Ar-you-eye-en," the diesel mate pronounces it letter by letter as he writes.

"It fits. Many thanks. Ruin—never thought of that."

The moment I'm back on the bridge I'm sent down the tower hatch again.

Mastheads have been spotted: a solitary steamer. By following a parallel course just out of its sight, we can determine its speed and tacking pattern. Instead of the usual four-man watch, there are six men up on the bridge: it is particularly important at this point to be on guard against surprise attack.

The commander has decided to have a go. "Clear the bridge! Flood and proceed at periscope depth!" is his first command. As always, as I scramble down the tower shaft I'm hampered by the camera. I wish it were small enough to go into my trouser pocket. Already the signal is flashing that the diesels are ready for the dive. The boat goes under.

In the control room, the chief is sitting with the two hydroplane operators, intent on hydroplane controls, depth gauges, and trimming gauges—surrounded by a mind-boggling profusion of tangled cables, gray-and-red hand wheels, white dials, scales, and indicators. The boat's power and its movements are incarnated in the interaction of needles and gauges.

The control room mate squats next to the chief, ready to turn the hand wheels of the air distributors.

The ventilators are switched off. At once, an overpowering stench of fuel, sweat, and bilge. The atmosphere condenses rapidly into wisps of vapor.

The sudden silence is oppressive. Only the soft hum of the E-motors, as if from a great distance, and the thin shock of water dripping somewhere into the bilge. A shudder runs through the boat like a gust of cold air.

The commander doesn't have much faith in his surface telescopic target marker; a layer of putty had come loose in the lens system during a depth charge attack on the previous voyage. The damage has not been properly repaired in dock. The miserable weather clinches his decision to opt for a periscope attack because the periscope captures more light.

In the control room, the two men at the hydroplane controls have now been joined by the control room mate, by the chief, who's in charge of the trim, and of course by the commander himself. The first watch officer is crouching by the calculator up in the tower, feeding it data on the enemy ship's position. The lead computed by the calculator is automatically fed into the gyro-steering mechanism of the torpedoes, which is continually adjusted up to the very moment of ejection.

The commander's voice: "Follow alongside!"

An extra adjustment mechanism ensures that the course the torpedo must follow in order to hit its target is constantly corrected. Not until the torpedo is fired will the pivot disconnect itself.

Another command: "Port fifteen—come to thirty degrees—slow ahead!"

The commander shows no sign of excitement. Now he even condescends to comment: "We're well set, chief. Let's gain a little more." Then, reverting to his usual tone of authority: "Go to forty feet, please! Periscope still under water."

The commander turns from the waist to speak across his shoulder, as casually as though this were just another exercise: "To the radioman: Nothing to be seen apart from the one vessel which is now on our port side astern. There's still time for a sonar search!"

Now he raises his chin and directs his voice up the tower, articulating each word with clipped precision: "First watch officer—if we happen to come across something to chew on today, we can probably manage with a double shot . . . but just in case . . ." At this point the commander raises his voice and calls out briskly, "Tubes one to four stand by for under-water firing. Flood tubes. Open torpedo doors!"

Acknowledgments from up front like echoes.

The radioman, now acting as sound man, delivers his report: "Propeller noise at two hundred and twenty degrees—sound bearing steady—quite loud—no other noise."

The chief's report—"Boat balanced"—sounds almost absent-minded. He is obviously intent on achieving as composed a front as that of the commander. The commander fingers his beard, then suddenly raises his head and shouts up the tower, "Switch on tubes one and two."

Now he looks straight at me and says: "Let's have a go, then—what time?"

"Fifteen thirty-five," replies the navigator.

At last the commander ups the periscope and grapples with its massive shaft, looking for all the world like a dancing bear. He's searching intently in the area where we assume the enemy to be.

As time ticks by without a word from him, I look questioningly at the chief. But he just shrugs his shoulders.

The commander is barely rotating the periscope at all now, and murmurs: "To the radio shack—just once more, an exact bearing!"

I am about to repeat his words, in case the sound man hasn't heard, when the report comes back:

"Two hundred and twenty-five degrees—getting rapidly louder—moving forward."

"I see," says the commander and looks in the specified direction.

"Quite exciting," murmurs the chief.

In lieu of a reply, I clear my nose, inhaling noisily. The commander pushes the periscope a little farther up. Suddenly his voice brightens: "There she goes! Quite a nice scow! Fucking awful weather. She can't be tacking, can she? Well, I'll be damned! That is exactly what she's doing. Tacking, so help me!"

The commander detaches his face from the rubber shell, pulls in the periscope, and turns to us: "Range twelve thousand feet! Go to zero! Half speed ahead." And to the mate in the tower: "Prepare for comparison reading. Enemy position bow right—angle sixty—enemy speed eleven knots. It looks as though we'll have to fire a spread. Dispersal at an angle of three degrees!"

Thereupon, speaking to me: "With shitty visibility like this I don't even bother to look for planes. They're gone before you even catch sight of them!"

For two long minutes nothing happens. We stand about like the Pyramids. At last, the commander opens his mouth again: "What sonic bearing?"

"Two hundred and seventy-five degrees," is the sound man's instant reply.

The commander turns slightly toward the chief engineer. "Chief, can I give 'slow ahead' and up the periscope?"

The chief nods eagerly. He looks incapable of getting a single word out for the tension. But then at last I hear him say: "Yessir."

The commander turns the periscope to 275 degrees, then pushes it gently upward. This time we don't have to wait. As soon as the eyepiece clears the water, he cries: "Got her!"

He shifts the periscope an inch or two. He does not seem to think that a last look around is required. Indeed, he pulls the periscope back down: "We're almost there!" we're informed.

But the moment he ups the periscope again, he starts grumbling and cursing.

Apparently the steamer has taken to zigzagging once more. Could the crew on the steamer have caught sight of our periscope? The sky periscope is bulkier than the attack periscope and so it stirs up more foam; it is shorter, too, and therefore there is a greater danger that the boat might break the surface on account of some mistake in the trim. There have been instances of boats engaged on a periscope attack being rammed by an abruptly turning steamer. That's precisely what happened to Commander Endrass in 1941. But the weather was probably even worse on that occasion.

"Coming straight, " I hear the commander mumble. If only he would give us a regular running commentary! How can one possibly form a picture of what is going on just on the basis of his curses and grumbles. I wish we had one of those well-known radio reporters at the periscope—someone who talks too much.

From time to time the commander goes into a half-crouch—not exactly the most comfortable of positions. And now he even moves around the periscope with bended knees, looking extremely awkward. He'd be better off at the sky periscope, where there's a seat like a motorbike saddle for him to sit on with the massive shaft between his knees, a seat he can set spinning just by stepping on a pedal.

The navigator's face has set into a mask. In his left hand he holds a clipboard, in his right a stopwatch.

"That's it—nice and broadside," murmurs the commander.

He spins in a circle for a look all the way around. You never know, there could be a destroyer lurking. Solitary steamers like these trundling all on their own across the seascape can conceivably be there as bait.

The tension is such that I haven't even heard whether the tubes have been reported ready for action. Bound to have been, I tell myself.

The commander ups periscope once more. After a good two minutes of intense observation, he says: "Look at that—zigzagging again! But not that much, really—more or less exactly what we need! Range approximately one thousand five hundred. Chief, a double shot from one and two. Can we do that at half speed?"

"You bet, Herr Kaleunt! No problem."

"To the tower!" The commander has raised his voice: "Enemy course twelve

knots—torpedoes to sixteen feet—hydroplane station—bow right—angle fifty—follow changing angle!"

I can clearly hear the calculator purring, as it transmits the new periscope direction and the lead to the deadly eels.

The tension is overwhelming. I only wish I could have one look through that periscope.

The litany of orders continues:

"To the tower: enemy angle seventy-five—keep on following!"

The commander's voice did not drop the way it usually does on the last word. That tells me there's more to come. Sure enough: "Tubes one and two ready to fire! Half speed ahead! Chief, the depth is fine!"

I notice the chief's left chin muscle twitch. His mouth remains firmly clamped. This is no time to bask in praise from the Old Man.

The commander's whole body is arched forward with such tension that he looks as if he were trying to force his head right into the metal of the periscope.

"Tube one!" he says, his voice unusually harsh in the silence. A measured pause, and then, just as harshly: "Fire!"

I instantly feel the slight jolt caused by the ejection of a torpedo, even as I hear the commander say: "Tube two—fire!"

I've got it: we haven't fired a spread after all, but two eels on a parallel course—one after the other, though, so there's a shift in the target.

The radioman reports: "Both torpedoes on their way!"

At once we flood to make up for the loss of weight.

We surface. We show ourselves, the treacherous fish rearing its head.

I have often asked myself, what can they be feeling, the men aboard a doomed vessel, when our streaming tower emerges suddenly in an eddy of frothing water, when the tip of our bow pierces the surface, when the gray shark plows up a ring of foam, when our heads, bristling with binoculars, appear above the bulwark . . . Hatred? Horror? Paralysis?

The stern of the tanker torn apart by a torpedo explosion drifts away from the forecastle. The severed parts can sometimes stay afloat because tankers are frequently subdivided by watertight bulkheads.

I am up there hard on the commander's heels and get a fix on our target at once: our torpedo has hit the steamer amidships. The eviscerated vessel's bow and stern reach heavenward for an instant. Then they totter, fall back. The ship appears grotesquely elongated, as though it were of stretched rubber. The two halves drift farther and farther apart.

"It's crazy," says the commander. "Bow's holding out . . . so's the aerial."

We have a clear view of two lifeboats being hoisted out from the stern. But we can also see people standing on the forecastle. And that section seems to have neither lifeboats nor rafts.

"Let's have a wander around the whole mess," says the commander, and gives corresponding rudder and engine orders.

During our maneuver the two halves of the ship stop moving. The aerial is still holding.

"We'll have to put some holes in it for the air to go through!" says the commander. "Man battle stations on the upper deck!"

"Come on, hurry!" blurts the bosun. He could have saved his breath: the men come scrambling up at top speed.

In days past I used to ask myself what could be the point of such pitiless artillery bombardment—after all, the ship was lost anyhow. Now I know that English rescue tugs venture out on hair-raising missions to haul whatever portions of wrecks manage to stay afloat into West Coast harbors. It is always cheaper to put a ship together from a bow and a stern than to build a new one from scratch. And a ship's aesthetics are no longer something that matters to our foe.

The catastrophe which overtook the hunted ship is rendered in our war log in the most laconic terms:

12:32. Tanker sighted. Two torpedoes fired. Both are hits. Tanker cracks immediately. Heavy smoke caused by explosion.

15:10. Surfaced. Tanker laboring in rough seas. Breaks where hit. Crew into four boats, one raft. Both parts of the wreck stay afloat. Bridge up in flames. Tanker *Clea* 7987. Guns astern. On each arm of the bridge, a round armored observation post with slits.

16:10. Artillery into action. 83 rounds at both parts of the vessel. Stern section sunk at 16:59. Forecastle vertical, but letters of name still visible above water. Fired MGC/30 at forecastle. Side pierced. Air expelled slowly from compartments.

In fact, the forecastle section was not submerged totally until 17:30.

Usually, we fire from a greater distance—our target, steamers that seem no more than shadows. It helps to keep the imagination under control. But when it's like this? What will happen to those poor devils in the lifeboats? And that couldn't have been the whole crew anyhow. The men on the forecastle will surely have been taken off by their pals in the boats—but what of the others? Did they stay by their cauldrons and burn? What can the scene have been in the engine room when the torpedoes came crashing against the brittle side, so precisely on target, exploding their charges?

I have to check my imagination, slipping like a runaway anchor chain, and swallow the rising lump in my throat.

"Scrap metal business," murmurs the commander.

I can see only one side of his face. It is absolutely closed: no more of the enthusiasm that was generated by the discovery of the prey. The hunting fever, too, has subsided. The laborious kill is like a blow in the kidneys.

What does a steamer look like after sinking six or eight thousand feet? What happens to boats like ours when they can no longer be kept from drowning? Are the wrecks crushed into huge compact lumps? Or do the compartments and the ruptured pressure hull flood so quickly with water that the pressure outside and in is soon equalized? Do they therefore retain their shape as they sink onto the seabed?

And what happens to the men sunk along with their ships? Do corpses gradually rot in the lower depths? Are there fish that far down, to gnaw the flesh off their bones? There's no one to talk to about such things, no one to provide hard information.

Nothing is said either about the fate of the shipwrecked survivors. To rescue them is forbidden. Our orders are unambiguous. Submarine High Command issued a classified message "For Officers Only" to each and every boat: "No survivors are to be taken on board. We have to be hard in this war!"

Instead of organizing a celebration in the officers' mess, the commander is brooding in the control room. I know from the others that he usually reacts this way. For an old sailor like him, any steamer with its thumping heart of steel is a living creature with its own biography, its own character.

The commander tries to dispel the uneasiness by factual explanations: "When the relative bearing indicator on a periscope fails, the orders for the torpedo setting have to be passed down by the torpedo officer—in this case the first watch officer—through the speaking tube or by messenger. Under such circumstances you have to dispense with an angle shot, in order to prevent any error in the course of your eel. So that leaves you with a straight shot as your only option. . . ." The commander hesitates, so I look him straight in the face like an attentive pupil listening to his teacher. "The calculated lead," he continues promptly, "is then allowed for on the lower socket of the dial, and the periscope is set accordingly. You let go the moment the target point swings by. This is more or less how it works: I let the watch officer have the data as I observe them, he passes down the indicated lead, the navigator adjusts the bearing index and reads off five degrees by five degrees how far I must still let the boat turn, that is, how far the target is moving through the

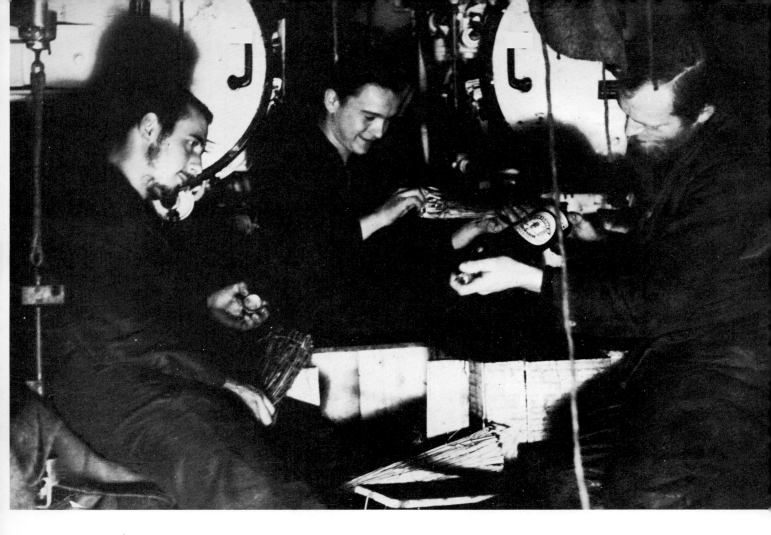

The men in the bow compartment, of whom only the members of the gun crew have seen the sinking with their own eyes, are openly jubilant: their boat will not now return empty-handed, as it did on the previous trip. Besides, there is now more space in the U-room: two torpedoes are gone. There's a special ration of beer—half a bottle each.

Many of the sailors in these pictures are beardless. It should not be thought that they have shaved. They are too young as yet to grow one.

adjusted bearing. This makes the torpedo proceed directly along the heading. The lead corresponds in fact to the angle between the periscope target line and the course of the boat. You have to be careful that the torpedo doesn't go charging out with a double lead error. That can easily happen—all it takes is for you to mix up 'bow left' and 'bow right.' "

The commander is staring straight ahead, as though listening to the sound of his own voice, then he adds: "By the way, if you're aiming like that, with the whole boat as it were, you also give the bow compartment the order: 'Zero angle.' It's all very simple."

Later on, the commander confides: "It's never pleasant, a hit like that. You know only too well what devastation it wreaks on the ship, and in that moment your enemy is no longer a foe, but some poor fellow who ought somehow to be given help. We used to get close, to provide the lifeboats with water, food, and a fix on their position. Even then we couldn't transmit their position over the radio, because that would have given our own position away to the enemy's anti-submarine defense forces. But now everything, absolutely everything, has gone by the board."

Other commanders—usually they were younger than ours—went so far as to boast of their victories over the radio. Thus, U-37 reported on one occasion:

> Today before Gibraltar/two scows on the submarine altar.
> Escaped a Tommy trap/nine hours of hellish flap.
> Fuel running low/home as fast as we can go.

The High Command expressed its approval: "This radio signal reflects the proper spirit."

In the west, a few clouds are still swathed in reddish light. They stand out against the sky like gangrenous sores. The water beneath them glitters with red beads. Gradually, the entire expanse of sky turns that malevolent shade of red associated with wine stains on white tablecloths. Then suddenly all the reds are drained from the sky and the spangles vanish.

The moon is already high. There is so much light that on deck every slit is visible in the gratings. Forecastle and waves are robbed of all their color: the moonlight has translated everything into shades of black and white.

We trail an impressive train of foam in our wake. It gleams with a sheen of silver—but only for a short stretch. The effervescent bubbles which lend such sparkle to our wake vanish into nothing in the twinkling of an eye.

The earth encourages man's belief that it will treasure the traces of his existence for all time. The sea offers no such illusion: before our very eyes it wipes away our footprints.

When the moon breaks momentarily through the headlong rush of clouds, wispy braids of silver ripple across the dark waters. As the moonlight flickers, the waves are transformed from jagged silhouettes into silver-veined slopes of astonishing plasticity, strewn with moon currents, moon glitter, furrows of moon shadow. This gleaming, streaming, and rippling of silver is quite incomparable. It is not of this world. Our rush and roar and thunder provide a worthy accompaniment—the sounds, too, are unearthly.

The following morning, a wall of clouds bars the horizon. It climbs higher and higher into the sky, halfway toward the zenith, at which point it disintegrates into puffballs which scatter across the whole of the westerly sky.

Soon it is getting noticeably darker again. The suction and friction of gusting winds ruffle the water greedily. The roar of the sea gains in volume until it is one single vibrating sound mingling with the wailing of the wind.

The wind howls a steady, high-pitched howl; sometimes it breaks shrilly, only to revert to its former voice.

Whiplash after whiplash of squalling showers.

Later on, puddles of blue open in the sky, but there's no chance that the weather will improve while the wind continues blowing from the northwest.

By noon the sky is gray and chill once more. The wind has picked up speed. The sea is a gigantic range of breakers. Individual waves are not yet all that

high, but every single one curves and smashes. Thus mottled gray and white, the sea looks suddenly grizzled with age.

The storm slaps our faces with sharp blows of flying spray. Again and again the watch officer shouts: "Hold fast—Attention—Zero!" Which means: crouch down behind the bulwark and cling on for dear life. The water crashes down on our hunched backs and rushes up gurgling around our legs, pulling at them, until it finds an outlet and drains away. We are all long since soaked to the skin. But we keep having to straighten up again, forswearing the protection of the bulwark, to scan the sea and sky for any possible prey or pursuer, for steamers or destroyers.

At dinnertime we have to turn up the guard rails on the table and try to keep the soup from slopping over. If this state of affairs continues, we'll soon get nothing but cold cuts.

"Quite uncommon. Must be an oscillating North Atlantic storm front," is the commander's comment.

Before clambering on deck the following day, I really muffle up: work togs, leather gear, a duffel coat, plus rubber pants and a rubber jacket on top.

It has grown bitterly cold. We are almost within sight of the south coast of Iceland.

I fasten my sou'wester with a double knot under the chin. Now I am armed to face the weather. But I have no protection for my camera. It really needs a watertight casing. Again I'll have no choice but to keep licking the saltwater off the lens every few minutes, because the leather rag merely succeeds in smudging it.

The tower hatch is shut. Camera in hand, I have to balance precariously on the aluminum ladder directly beneath the heavy steel lid until my ears tell me there's no water gurgling overhead. Then I push the hatch open with my elbows and work my way up.

The storm comes racing in a sudden assault from a bad weather front straight ahead, tearing strips of white and green skin off the waves. There's a hissing and a roaring, as though waterfalls were being sent hurtling down the sides of tapped blast furnaces. The breakers are running higher and higher, gaining force all the time. The boat shoots up the slopes, projects its bow searchingly into the void, and immediately dives back into the green flesh of the sea. Another wall of water approaches, higher than any that have gone before. The wall turns transparent until it is gleaming like sheer green glass. Bearing its crown of foam, it is advancing directly to meet us. And now the bow pierces the wall and shatters it—and it comes crashing down upon our hunched backs and buries the entire boat.

The commander gives the order to dive, so that we can eat our lunch in relative peace. But within two hours we have to surface again. After all, we're here to sniff out the foe. At once the sea recovers its grip on the boat.

What a spectacle: the air is clear and hard as crystal. There are even a number of white clouds in the sky. The mist of flying spray skims the breakers, no more. The sea is now a speeding panorama of deep valleys and voluminous green hills.

The second watch officer and the forward starboard lookout.
The boat is making straight for a bad weather front.

Every time the bow emerges from the green waters and shakes off its swirling white load, it hoists a gleaming flag of water to leeward as though in triumph. Our watertight forecastle gives it this victorious buoyancy despite the most punishing blows.

Regardless of the trouncing I have to endure, I'm euphoric: no captain of a steamer has ever seen anything like this. We do not look down onto the sea, but up out of it, enveloped in water, like swimmers. Whenever we are pulled down into its valleys, we have to stretch our heads up and back: we see with the eyes of the sea.

Notwithstanding the violence of the storm and sea, we are perfectly safe: our vessel has no superstructure the breakers can crush. It lets itself ride, it side-steps every blow like a boxer and is instantly ready to face whatever is coming next.

These VII-C boats are unsinkable. They may not have the broad forecastle and stern needed to parry the rocking and sawing of the water—indeed their external stability is particularly precarious because the gap between the pressure hull and the fairing has water running through it—but the resilience of this type of boat is nevertheless phenomenal, thanks to its exceptionally low center of gravity. The ballast keel full of iron bars brings the boat back easily from the most perilously inclined positions as though it were a tumbler-doll.

And though the buoyancy is minimal when such a boat rides the surface—only a hundred and fifty tons, equal to the contents of a single trimming tank—it can proceed at top speed even in gale-force winds, precisely because its reduced surfaces offer the sea no resistance. Only the little round tower is exposed to its blows. The main body of the boat is low-slung in the water.

Even when the breakers come side-on, we need not be afraid. Even then nothing dreadful can happen to the boat, because the water cannot get inside it to fill up the compartments. The tower hatch stays shut whenever the weather is bad.

Particular care is required only when diving obliquely in stormy seas. In theory, the breakers could "knock down" the boat just as it's being flooded. When the boat is in that position, it may plunge downward through the surface of the sea too quickly, because the suction effect in the rise and fall of the water is greater when the boat is parallel to the mountainous waves than when it is head-on.

But as long as we face up to the sea as a surface vessel, we can feel totally secure.

We have to attach ourselves with safety belts: it has been known to happen that an entire watch was swept from the bridge by a monumental wave without anyone inside the boat being aware of their plight, because the tower hatch was clamped down, as always in such weather.

For those on bridge duty, the dictum "water is pointed" is a tangible experience. It penetrates through the tightest stitching. All it needs is time to make a mockery of the most rigorous precautions by working its way under the "waterproofs" to the skin and running down the chest and back. And our seaboots are wrongly designed besides: open at the top like any ordinary boot, they accumulate water until it squelches its way to overflowing.

Our faces are whipped to a garish red, because we keep having to turn them directly into the flying spray. Our eyes are smarting, with crusts of salt forming in the corners and all around the mouth. Our hands grow clammy from gripping the bridge's armor-plating.
Whenever a breaker roars in from aft, we are instantly submerged to the waist, with the water dragging us off balance.

In order to capture the stormy sea on film—the most marvelous vision our venerable Earth has to offer—I have to hold the camera into saltwater foam and flying spray. Later I discover that the storm has engraved its own image on the photographs in the form of drops and smudges.

How monstrous the power must be that can pile up the water into such foam-capped mountains and carve out such deep valleys!

The boat is carried high on a gigantic crest. I glance over the rolling waves as if over an endlessly meandering herd of animals. Diagonally beamed squalls skirt it like windblown draperies. At times the breakers resemble primeval mountain ranges of slate cut loose from their foundations and come to life; at others they look like the manes of madly stampeding horses.

Two days like this. While the westerly winds blow, there's no letting up: narrow horizons, a flat charcoal-gray sky, wailing squalls, careering clouds, flying spray that drenches us to the marrow of our bones. Now the breakers are coming obliquely from astern. We are not consulted, after all, regarding the course assigned to us on an outpost patrol. Again and again our stern shoots up, the white-crested gray-greenish breakers come rushing past from abaft on a level with the top of the bridge guard, flooding the foreship and submerging it entire, long as it is. The tower hatch still can't be kept open.

The following day the weather gets still worse. The gale and the swell increase yet another notch or two, until one can hardly distinguish between the sea and the sky: the elements of air and water are fused. This is what there must have been prior to the Creation: raging chaos.

Extreme demands are made on those manning the bridge. Four hours at a stretch on this springboard with tin walls are more than flesh and blood can bear. That is why the commander orders each stint to be halved.

Though our engines are running at two thirds ahead we cover no distance. We're only just holding our own against the sea. If we wanted actually to move ahead, it would mean even more fuel down the drain.

There is a considerable danger that we could be taken by surprise. Eventually, the commander relents and gives the order to dive.

A collective sigh of relief goes through the boat. All I want is to sprawl out and turn up my toes. Deliverance at last! My knotted muscles relax. At last, a floor we can keep our feet on again. At two hundred feet we are safe from the mauling of the waves.

The diesel engines are stopped. In the control room two of the exhausted and totally drenched bridge guards have sat down at the hydroplanes—the diving maneuver begins.

Overleaf: Meals can now be properly served in the bow compartment. The men don't have much of an appetite. They are slumped at the table or stretched out on their bunks, too exhausted to think of anything other than taking advantage of every minute of blessed peace.

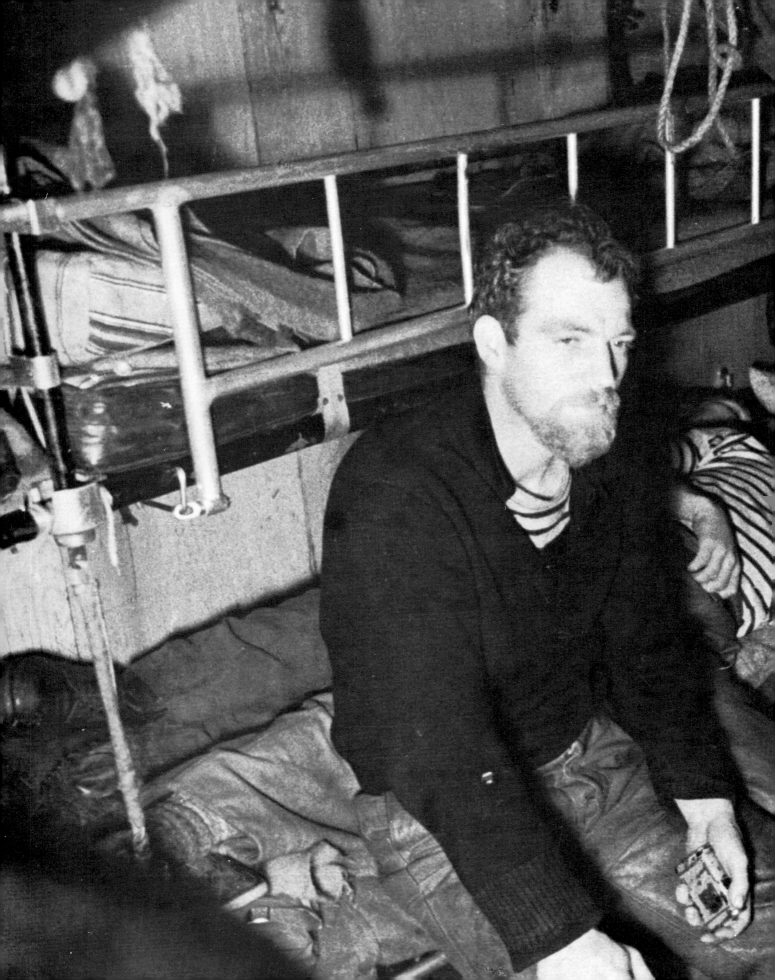

In an instant when the bridge is relatively dry, the tower hatch is pushed open from below: the commander comes up and tells the second watch officer to show him where. "Well, I'll be damned!" he growls after a while from behind the binoculars. "A German U-boat, that's for sure! They're not diving? Hell, they couldn't be diving, could they? Do they think we're English? Quick, get the signal flags up."

The commander yells rudder and engine orders down the funnel of the speaking tube. Our boat veers and heels over in the process. Spray and foam lash our heads—but no one is in the mood to duck right now. A huge wave comes at us from behind—an entire snow-capped Alpine range. It is hissing so loudly that we can't even hear ourselves speak. We are only half carried away by it; the bulk rolls past beneath our keel. But then it builds up ahead of us into an endless barrier cutting off our view. For some time now we've seen no sign of the others. Then the dark shape appears suddenly between the snow-topped peaks, like a cork popped from a bottle, and it's emitting flashes of light: long—short—long short—short—long: the predetermined signal by which we recognize one another. Over there they have heaved a portable searchlight up to the bridge, and they signal across through the mist and the foam until the boat is thrust down.

The commander wedges himself higher against the armor plating, standing on the iron foot rest. Someone is hanging on to him by one thigh for all he's worth. As the other boat comes up again, he spells out: "M-A-I-N-T-A-I-N-C-O-U-R-S-E-A-N-D-S-P-E-E-D-A-M-C-O-M-I-N-G-A-L-O-N-G-S-I-D-E!"

Together with the signal flags, they've handed up my camera, as requested. I too must heave myself up higher. The second watch officer gropes beneath my rubber jacket and holds me by my belt. One of the bridge guards leans heavily against my legs.

At that moment, a mountain of water even huger than any that has come before bears down on us. Out of the corner of my eye I see the corrugated foam-flecked flank and the white cloud whirling from its crest. It takes my breath away.

"Attention—Zero!" roars the commander, and the second watch officer hauls me down. I cower clinging with all my might to the direction finder. I try to make myself as bulky as possible and to be a dead weight, meanwhile pressing the camera hard against my belly with the lens turned inward for protection.

Too much is too much! This has to be more than even the boat can take.

With bated breath I count several heartbeats, and then in every fiber of my body I feel the stern being pushed up, a heavy blow from abaft crashes with a hollow sound against the tower, and as I peer from behind my raised left arm, I can see a frothing whirlpool rush right into the bridge. The raging waters tug and tear at my legs—I stagger and they almost bring me down. Spreading my elbows, I wedge myself in between the periscope housing and the armor-plating—before long I manage to pull my feet up above the level of the whirlpool. Now I dare to raise my eyes and look ahead: the giant wave shows us its backside, as it rolls across the foreship. The foreship is so totally submerged that there appears to be none at all, as though we had gone to sea in a tower and nothing else.

*Flag signals are addressed
across the breakers to
the other boat.*

Overcome at the sight of the other boat's tower emerging from the boiling sea, the second watch officer starts whooping with delight. The others wave across until the boat disappears as though by magic.

Such meetings of two boats in mid-Atlantic are rare, particularly in the midst of a raging storm. To please me, the commander maneuvers us up close. The commander, who had served on training clippers before the war and who understands the seas, winds, and weather like no one else, explained later on why this maneuver had not been reckless: "In theory, the sea is just like a cornfield with a wind blowing through it." That is not exactly true; on the surface there are certain permutations—as you can see by watching the ears of corn. You just have to know what they amount to.

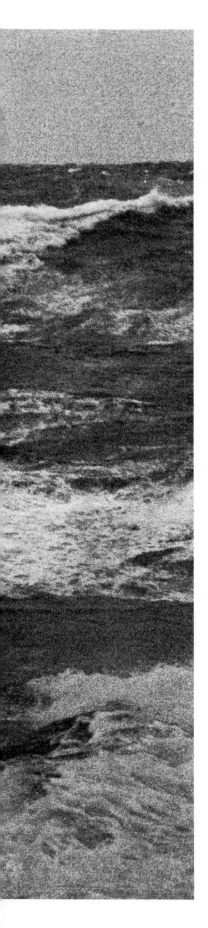

The boat is still veering. The commander decides to go the whole hog. There's no other vessel that would allow him even to try such a maneuver. But this type of submarine has always come out right side up. Not one has ever capsized.

We make our way laboriously through the grinding millstones of water toward the other boat. But now the breakers are coming abeam. Time and time again the bridge tilts at such an angle that we almost spill out. It is out of the question for me to have another go at climbing higher.

Our bow is aimed squarely at the middle of the other boat. At times it seems to be trapped forever in the waves, but then it manages to dig itself out and poises for a few seconds, reaching steeply into the void, until it rushes downward again and is buried in its own fall. The boat is staggering, shaken and wrenched. The bow tries to bolt sideways, as though this could shake off its burden.

In the haze of flying spray, the other boat is nothing but a diffused gray silhouette which suddenly disappears altogether and remains out of sight for minutes, only to reappear just as suddenly up close, diagonally below us. From where I am, I can look down into their bridge. Every single bridge guard is recognizable. Their pale faces are turned toward us, open-mouthed—they look like baby birds in their nest. The hissing of the bursting waves as they thrash against our tower is so deafening that the other crew's yells are reduced to mere silent mouthings. They must be terrified to see us hanging here so dangerously close above them.

As we swing around, we're coming closer and closer to the other boat. High seas are tossed aside by our bow as though by a snowplow and collide with seas from their boat coming athwart us. A ragged mass of water gushes straight up into the air like a geyser. We're on a collision course for sure.

"Made to measure!" I hear someone bellowing close to my ear.

"Let's hope they're not making a film over there!" That was the commander. Isn't he tempting fate? Is he still not going to order the rudder reversed?

There's a flurry of waving over there. The commander shouts straight into my face: "That's Hirsacker—U-Five-Seventy-two."

Again, a wave carries us piggyback, and again we're on the way up. We soar skyward in the swinging seat of a ferris wheel.

I lean out over the armor plating. At once I'm struck in the face by flying foam. I press the release, wind the film on, lick the lens and point my camera diagonally downward. All this time I'm being clamped in the second watch officer's iron grip.

My Heavenly Assumption comes to an end and I sink back exhausted.

I glance at the commander's face. His lips have a mocking curl to them, which immediately cuts me down to size, and leaves me full of admiration. "Will that do? Pictures good enough?" he shouts.

Pray God the shutter didn't jam! Nobody has ever seen anything like it: blizzard-spouting volcanoes, whole mountain ranges alive and moving—and in the midst of it all the other boat—a storm-tossed scrap of steel with a handful of men tied to the bridge.

Now the sea has let go of us again. With our boat almost standing on its head, we crash down into a valley of watery dust—down and down.

Far above us through the clouds of spray I suddenly catch sight of the tip of

the other boat's bow and then the topmost rim of its tower. Now they are up and we are down. Now they can see us as we saw them a moment ago. Once again; point the camera and press the release. No idea how much film I've exposed. There's no time to bother about that.

Then the other boat is gone again. I sink down behind the armor plating, can no longer see anything, can only hear the waves, the thundering breakers, the wicked hissing of the air bubbles, and the resounding blows against the body of the boat. When I have recovered my strength sufficiently to get up again, the other boat looks like a barrel tossing into the air and then sinking back into the foam.

The barrel gets smaller and smaller. Now it is no bigger than a dancing cork. Another couple of minutes and it has vanished for good. The commander shouts steering orders down the speaking tube. We revert to our former course.

After a little while the commander says: "It really makes you wonder—so few boats in the Atlantic—and here we're having a real party!"

I know what he means: Strategic Command can't be coping too well.

Two days later in the course of dinner the commander says:

"We've heard from Hirsacker."

"Where is he, if one may ask?"

"Just east of the Azores."

I try to visualize the sea chart: U-572 must have gone almost due south. Very mysterious. What a pity we didn't ask.

Preceding double spread: This photo showing a VII-C boat from above is commonly assumed to have been taken from the air. But this is not true. Nor did I use a telescopic lens. It was simply taken from the bridge of our U-96, as it was lifted high above the other boat by a gigantic wave.

Here the other boat moves away due south after our meeting in the eye of the storm. Its commander at this time was Kapitänleutnant Hirsacker. He was condemned to death by military tribunal in 1943. The charge: "Cowardice in the face of the enemy." The boat (U-572) was lost under Oberleutnant Kummetat, bombarded from the air northeast of Trinidad on August 3, 1943.

The navigator is one of the most important men aboard, responsible as he is for ensuring that the boat reaches its area of operations as rapidly as possible. He doesn't have the chart house you would find on a steamer, but has to work within the close confines of the control room, amid switches, pipes, gauges, and valves, surrounded by activity. His work space is a table measuring only about three feet by five. His sea charts are stowed in the large metal chest which doubles as a seat for the hydroplane operators. The most important tools of his trade are his two sextants, his celestial globe, his nautical tables, and almanacs. German navigators are given such nicknames as "Semiversus," "Sinus," "Kosinus," and "Azimuth Fiddler."

Our navigator—like most—is a very prosaic fellow. He has no time at all for the beauties of the firmament. He takes an exclusively professional view of the sky and has a meteorological explanation to hand for every brightening or darkening, for every combination of colors. He is on intimate terms with the various constellations. When they are hidden from view by a veil of clouds, he suffers, waiting irritably for the call from the bridge: "Ready to take a sun sight!" or "Ready to take a star sight!"

Given the poor weather conditions in mid-Atlantic, the navigator is frequently prevented from getting an astronomic fix on our position. He must then rely on dead reckoning with whatever information he has on our course and speed. But the course record compiled from compass readings is not very reliable because currents and gales affect the boat.

The navigator takes the two sextants from their case in the control room. Then he climbs to the bridge. The control room mate hands the valuable instruments up to the helmsman, who passes them on.

"Stopwatch ready," the navigator calls down.

The navigator blinks as he gazes into the sunlight, then he raises the sextant and presses his right eye to the sight. He is seeing double—the actual sun and its reflection on the mirror which can be moved along the protractor. Now he fiddles with the set screw, until the mirror-image of the sun hits the horizon.

"Zero!" calls the navigator. Down in the control room, someone presses the button on the stopwatch and reads off the time span marked by the chronometer.

The navigator says not another word. After a while he repeats the rite.

From the rows of figures in his nautical tables, the navigator subsequently extracts the components of his formulas. These enable him to work out our coordinates. Where the two base lines intersect we have our boat's position.

The navigator can never relax. Aside from his ordinary duties, he is the third watch officer. If a convoy is sighted, he no longer has a minute to himself. Armed with graph paper, triangle, dividers, and stopwatch, he has to figure out what our speed and general course should be on the basis of reports coming down from the bridge. No simple matter, when a convoy is moving along in a pronounced zigzag.

The control room mate makes a note of our latest position on the sea chart. This shows the boat's travels in the form of an angular meandering line, interrupted every inch or so by an intersecting line, which carries an indication of the time of day. The distance between the lines of intersection corresponds to the distance covered by the boat in any four-hour period. From the size of the spaces between these lines of intersection one can see at a glance whether progress has been rapid or slow.

Ever since the convoy was spotted, the commander has not left the bridge. The clouds of smoke on the horizon can be joined at any moment by the menacing mastheads of escort vessels.

Next double spread: Despite the tension and the excitement of the chase, the routine aboard is undisturbed: men off duty having their meal in the bow compartment.

As in World War I, the enemy tries to safeguard his supplies by making sure that his cargo ships do not travel on their own but rather in convoy formation, protected by destroyers, corvettes, gunboats, and aircraft.

The very need to have the ships gather into convoys is a severe handicap in itself: freighters have to remain in port fully loaded, waiting for the convoy to assemble. During the crossing, the swifter vessels have to abide by the speed of the slowest. Great detours become necessary, to pick up vessels joining the convoy along the way. At rendezvous points, long waits are not unusual. And the ports of destination become overcrowded, obliged to cope with too many ships at once. This produces delays similar to those on departure.

The convoy consists of more or less serried columns. There are destroyers in the front, destroyers trotting up and down the flank like sheepdogs, and destroyers making up the rearguard. On occasion, additional escort vessels travel in between the files.

The destroyers accompanying a convoy are not only supposed to fight off any submarines attacking from outside or even inside the formation. They are supposed to prevent them from getting anywhere near the convoy. That is why they are sent by day on far-flung security patrols to hold the submarines at bay or to make them stay submerged for long enough so that they cannot catch up with the convoy under cover of night. The aircraft that assist in these patrols make them even more effective.

The war log of the Naval High Command contains the following entry for July 11, 1941: "Those in charge of the convoys have learned a great deal since the beginning of the war. The British now direct their convoys quite unsystematically across the whole expanse of the Atlantic. The routes no longer follow any discernible pattern. Submarine successes are significantly down on account of the greater distances to be patrolled and of strengthened enemy defenses, but the Submarine Division consider that this unsatisfactory state of affairs is likely to be transitory."

We're patrolling yet another new beat. This frigging around is anything but restful. Even when I'm lying on my bunk, I can't relax. Every sense is in a

The bosun of the third watch has drawn the hated and troublesome sun sector.

constant state of alert. I can never fall into a really deep sleep: it is a cobweb veil which the slightest untoward sound will tear to shreds. It is further frayed by constant modifications of our accustomed background noise: the sound of the diesel engines is suddenly interrupted for repairs, then the engines start up again with a splutter, and the hiss and murmur of the sea gets abruptly louder. Then the tower hatch is opened and water comes splashing down. Then the ventilators start humming and the bilge pumps are put to work. The unmitigated tension is killing.

The chief is squatting on his bunk, engrossed in diagrams of switchboards and plans of pipes. There's something wrong somewhere. In his usual fashion—namely, with a paper clip he's twisted open—he traces the black and white outlines of the diagram. Then he absent-mindedly carves doodles into the green linoleum surface of the mess table.

The first watch officer is sitting next to him, polishing his binoculars and cultivating a calm and collected look.

Three flies are hovering around the lamp.

Suddenly the chief looks up to ask: "The book you're reading, what's it like?"

"Not bad—five dead so far!"

"Terrific! I'll put my name down." And he's back to his detective work.

Our horizon has the diameter of a thimble as compared to the circle an RAF reconnaissance plane can survey. In the early days, the weather did at least give us an occasional advantage. But no longer. The enemy is unaffected by poor weather conditions now. Radar works in all weather. Indeed, the situation is reversed: bad weather now gives the airplanes an added advantage. When they are navigating by radar our bridge guards spot them even later than otherwise. The planes can take our boats even more easily by surprise. And once a boat is unfit to dive, it has to be given up for lost, because there is no way we can come to its aid. Any little fault in the diving mechanism, a simple breakdown that could perhaps be repaired within a couple of hours, is sufficient to put our boats at the enemy's mercy. They are wide open to systematic destruction from the air. Not a single plane of ours will come to their rescue.

For the Tommies, the Atlantic is now their very own unchallenged playground. Our Air Force is out of it, once and for all. The RAF can afford to make use of their oldest birds, their worn-out Sunderlands. They can even approach the French coast without the slightest risk.

I'm up on the bridge to take a whole uninterrupted sequence of pictures of the watch and the pounding foreship. The third watch, the navigator's watch, happens to be on duty.

Suddenly this most circumspect of men turns on his heels, yells, "Convoy!" at me and reports downward: "To the commander: Smoke trail to starboard ninety degrees!"

The commander is on the bridge in an instant. I'm surprised that he hasn't left his cap behind in the hurry. The navigator must have shaken him out of his bunk ("Stockpiling sleep is a commander's first duty"). He devotes a good

The navigator has just
discovered the smoke trail and
is reporting its presence down
into the boat.

ten minutes to close observation, gives rudder and engine orders, then lowers the binoculars and scratches his beard with his free hand: he's working out his tactics. He asks the chief about our fuel reserves. He must be contemplating a long chase.

We're now running parallel to the convoy's estimated course. Conceivably, the convoy may be tacking right now. We'll know before long. The main thing is to figure out the convoy's general course and report it as soon as possible to Headquarters.

The commander takes us closer, until mastheads are visible and even for an instant a glimpse of smokestack.

"They're traveling without much smoke," says the commander. "Good work."

At that very moment, as though to mock him, a ball of smoke comes up from the convoy.

"Must be a tremendous convoy. Wide formation—staggered ranks—several columns. Five or six at least."

I can't see how the commander can deduce so much from so few clues.

"Right way around," he mumbles in my direction. I know what he means: a convoy going east—the ships are loaded. Let's hope it won't change its course.

"Probably coming from Halifax. They assemble near Halifax and head across way up here."

Long minutes of wordless tension. Then from the commander: "Prepare radio message!"

But he raises the binoculars to his eyes again and keeps his own counsel. None of us finds out what the text of the message is to be.

I can well imagine why the commander is hesitating. It's that nagging worry: if we emit a short signal now, however tiny the number of letters required to inform Headquarters of the convoy's course and speed, plus the weather conditions, we cannot by any means be certain, given the area we're in, that it will not be intercepted by land-based stations. The commander, as a seasoned skeptic, obviously shares that fear despite the official attitude that it is impossible to intercept such short signals.

The commander lowers the glasses and his face clearly reflects his struggle to make up his mind. We *must* keep Headquarters informed—there's no question about that.

A convoy is a rare find. Whenever one is spotted everything that can move must be brought in—Headquarters guides boats to the spot by radio over hundreds of sea miles. The worst thing that can happen is for contact to be lost once the pack is on its way.

Instead of "maintaining contact" we call it "sawing." Tracking a convoy, sawing away at it, means a laborious to and fro, tacking this way and that. It means that there'll be no sleep. Our battle readiness combines with a sense of anticipation to keep us awake: at some point we'll have to overcome the jitters, to "vanquish the coward within," or whatever one likes to call coping with fear.

A great deal is asked of a commander who attacks a convoy: fully aware of what is awaiting his boat, he is expected to charge ahead and unleash his fighting fish into the underworld—which is not unlike poking a walking-stick

Next pages: Again and again
the commander or one of the
watch officers climbs up on the
periscope base or stands on the
foot rests of the bulwark: every
foot they add to their height
increases their range of vision.
The perennial handicaps of the
submarine—its low vantage
point and narrow range of
vision—are particularly vexing
now. The boat has no masts
and provides no means for a
man to climb up higher and
see more.

into a hornet's nest. The enemy has a whole arsenal of defensive and offensive weaponry at his disposal: turret guns, anti-aircraft guns, pom-pom guns, new, heavy depth charges—and any amount of radar equipment, for both surface and under-water search. He has fully trained and seasoned specialists manning the equipment who have had a great deal of practice maintaining the intricate interplay between the various ships. The precious freighters and tankers are guarded by up to three separate security screens.

If the chase drags on, the tension does slacken somewhat. But all the surreptitious tearing about wears out your nerves: there can't be anyone who isn't scared of being raked with depth charges.

We rake the enemy; the enemy rakes us . . . there's a lot of raking in the Navy. Technical understatement—we're really good at that. "A carpet" is our domestic little euphemism for searching fire involving large numbers of depth charges. "A garden rake"—"a Persian carpet"—anything to avoid the pompous. For the most wearying kind of runaround we have the happy verb "to slouch," and for the ordeal we are faced with now, the similarly unheroic "to saw."

I memorize all I've ever learned about convoys: since a convoy's speed is determined by that of the slowest steamer, it tends to make slow progress. The tacking and constant deviations from the straightest course slow it down even further. A submarine traveling on the surface can move approximately twice as fast as the average convoy and is therefore capable of cutting in ahead into a favorable position for an ambush. It is precisely to prevent that from happening that the destroyers of the escort undertake their search missions. Even if they don't actually sight any submarines on these missions, they can still succeed in forcing the boats under water by their mere presence. Because its under-water speed is much lower the submarine can no longer keep up. Inevitably, it starts to lag behind and must then slouch forward again as best it can. The game can be repeated ad infinitum, until the submarine no longer has the slightest chance of catching up. Its chances diminish even more rapidly when the enemy has aircraft to deploy along with the destroyers.

The stalking will go on and on. I can climb down into the control room without worrying that I might miss anything up on the bridge. I make my way from there through the front hatch for a look at what's going on in the bow compartment.

There's the usual twilight. I can see the rails and the tackle overhead. Already there are two reserve torpedoes hanging from the rails. The dim light glances off their thick layers of grease. The whole compartment reeks of the stuff. The pulley chains are rattling.

The torpedo mate is standing by, together with his team of mechanics, beside the openings of the torpedo tubes, his ear close to the speaking tube, intent on any order that may come down from the bridge.

Here, too, nobody has the slightest idea of what is going on above. Like miners at the coal face, these men are totally cut off from the world around them.

The commander dispenses information all too sparingly over the loudspeaker system. Anyone not on the bridge has no means of knowing how close we are to the convoy. When we are ready to launch a torpedo, the men are hardly any the wiser. They never get to see the enemy—not even the shadow of his ships.

The hatch leading aft is open now. But seen from here, the control room is so far away that it might just as well not be there. My sheepskin jerkin, which I'd left hanging up to dry in the hydroplane compartment, turns out to be still damp, but happily I have a dry duffel coat left in my locker. So I put on my duffel coat and slip oilskins on top: there's still a lot of water coming over the side.

The commander's bunk is deserted. And he wasn't in the control room either. He must be back on the bridge. It will be a long time before he will get to sleep again. "A time and a place . . ." has always been his watchword.

Up above, the sky is much clearer than I would have expected. Just an occasional cloud skirting the horizon straight ahead of us. When I turn my head, I see that there are a few others, equally close to the horizon, at the back of us, white towers looking like square-riggers with full-blown sails.

"They're over there," the commander tells me, pointing to port with his head.

I focus my binoculars, strain my eyes but can see nothing.

When the commander notices that I'm still lost, he comes to my aid: "Just underneath and to the left of that very bright cloud."

At last I discover a dark patch on the horizon—or rather the barest trace of a dark patch. However much I scan that stretch of sky, I do not spot any mastheads, not even a single bristle. The horizon is as smooth as can be. A radio message is passed up.

"From Fischl," says the commander. "He's also maintaining contact, but with a different convoy. . . . To each his own!"

After a while we hear from the commander again: "We've missed our chance for a daylight attack. The moon is almost full. Have to wait for the moon to go down."

We are steering a hundred and twenty degrees. Our diesel engines are running at standard speed.

The navigator comes up and takes a sight off the insipid sun. This gives him his first baseline. Presently he will direct his sextant once more against the sun, and have the stopwatch time recorded in the control room below. An accurate fix on our position is very important now.

As soon as the navigator has done his job, the sun disappears behind streaky rain clouds. The weather gets rapidly worse. After all, only the devil would make our life easy. The commander, a confirmed fatalist, almost takes it for granted that the sky will dim, that the horizon will blur and then dissolve totally in the haze.

The nor'westerly wind has risen to force 5. The sky is increasingly overcast, visibility is deteriorating. The sea is getting up to 4 at least. The boat heels over sharply. The wind stirs up the groundswell that has outlasted the recent storm.

Ahead of us, the horizon subsides in a dark squall of rain. Our range of vision narrows rapidly. Our situation has suddenly become precarious. We could be surprised by a pursuer at any moment.

The commander turns up in the control room, wearing a worried look. The convoy has disappeared from view.

Is there nothing more we can do? The commander is struggling to make up his mind. Suddenly he raises his head and gives the order: "Rig for diving!"

The bridge watch comes down sopping wet. The watch officer shuts the heavy lid of the hatch and turns the hand wheel, securing it in place. The sound of the diesels stops, the ventilation and exhaust valves are shut off. The E-motors are shifted to the propeller shafts and start soundlessly to transmit the power stored in our batteries. Within seconds, all compartments report they are ready to dive.

"Flood!" orders the commander.

The men in the control room tear open the vents, and the air escapes from the diving cells in a hissing, thundering surge. Both hydroplanes are turned sharply downward. The boat becomes bow-heavy. The needle on the depth gauge starts to move. All at once the roar and bluster cease. The ensuing silence is broken by the order: "Go to ninety-five feet!"

A movement of the hydroplanes makes the boat stern-heavy. The last bubbles of air escape from the diving cells.

"Close air vents!" comes from the chief, who then orders the hydroplane operators to take us to the desired depth. The chase becomes lurking and listening. The sound of enemy engines and propellers carries farther under water than our range of vision on the surface.

The commander squats down in the passage next to the radio shack. The sound man has put on his listening gear and is trying to identify signs of an enemy presence in the sounds of the water around us. Again and again, the commander asks: "Any bearing?"

Almost an hour goes by like this. The commander moves back and forth between the chart table in the control room and the passage next to the radio shack.

Suddenly the sound man's expression changes: his eyes are tightly shut, his mouth goes tense—now he's pursing his lips as though he'd just bitten into a lemon. With scarcely controlled excitement he reports: "Sound bearing to sixty degrees—very faint!"

Then, the sound man starts almost imperceptibly. I can hear the menacing thunder coming at him without the benefit of listening gear: depth charges.

"They're raking somebody—what's the bearing now?"

The commander is squatting right next to me in the passage.

"Seventy degrees—moving ahead!"

With a voice that is uncharacteristically harsh, the commander orders: "Immediately to fifty degrees! Rig for surface!"

Now the sound man is the only one to receive messages from outside the confines of the boat. He keeps up a steady stream of reports.

The weather has deteriorated even further. Now low-slung rain squalls are darkening the horizon all around. Daylight is almost totally extinguished. Splashes of flying spray ripped off the waves by the wind now hang over the seascape in a pale haze.

Again and again waterfalls come hurtling down through the tower hatch: but it cannot be shut now—the enemy is too close.

An Alarm

The commander no longer even lowers the binoculars: our situation could not be more unpromising. He has to decide whether to order us down again, to guard the boat against any potential surprises coming out of the rain squalls, or whether to continue the blind advance against the enemy.

Suddenly I hear a voice come through the splashing, rushing turmoil: "Mastheads aft to starboard!"

"There we are!" says the second watch officer right next to me.

"Alarm!"

The commander has yelled the dreaded word down into the tower.

The men of the watch drop through the hatch. The commander is the last man in and pulls down the lid.

With a few leaps I reach the engine room. The red lights announcing the alarm down here are already flashing. The engine crew can communicate only through hand signals: as they go through their motions at lightning speed the fuel supply to the diesels is interrupted and the engines are disconnected. While the diesels grind to a halt, both E-motors are switched on farther aft.

My eyes and my camera are fixed sternward: the diesel stoker is standing between the two superchargers, spinning his hand wheels to shut the external exhaust vents, so that no water can get into the engines through the exhaust manifold, which will now be submerged.

All at once the men in the engine room, accustomed to a cavelike workshop atmosphere, find themselves in the thick of battle. When the alarm came the chief happened to be next to the E-motors. He has to get to the control room. I and my camera are in the way. There's no room here for photographers. With both E-motors going at full speed and obeying the pressure exerted by the hydroplanes, which are turned downward fore and aft, the boat makes its bow-heavy descent. The hydroplane pressure pulls down the bow and pushes up the beam—at this particular speed it swoops down like a fighter plane.

The boat is still bow-heavy. The bilge water comes rushing forward beneath the floor plates.

At the sound of "Alarm!" the second watch officer comes tumbling down.

Alarm in the engine room. Thank goodness I happen to have loaded a fast film. These must be the only unsimulated photographs ever taken in such a situation. The men, who have no idea what is going on, could easily be driven mad by apparently contradictory orders, were it not for their excellent training and their experience. They hear the bells go off, see the alarm signals flash, hear the engine telegraph spring into action, see sudden changes in what it indicates. The order to blow out the diving tanks with diesel fumes comes by telephone. That at least gives them some idea. They can only guess what the implications may be of the stream of other orders. The control room is so far away that it might as well not exist.

"Go to periscope depth!" orders the commander from his vantage point in the tower.

The chief orders: "Balance the boat!"

Both hydroplanes are reversed, then the boat is brought onto an even keel. The last remnants of air have been driven out of the diving cells.

The water column in the Papenberg is sinking, which indicates that the boat must be rising.

The commander still cannot see a thing through the periscope in the tower. His voice reveals impatience: "Request depth." At that very moment the periscope clears the water. The chief shouts upward into the tower: "Boat balanced!"

No one says a word. At last the commander, in a hushed voice: "To hydrophone projector: Destroyer on the starboard beam!"

Is the commander intending to attack the destroyer—right now? In broad daylight?

Minutes go by. Then the commander's voice comes again: "Flood tubes one to four!"

Such silence reigns within the boat that the command sounds deafening.

Soon the voice from heaven comes again, more gently: "To control room: Chief engineer, hold our exact depth!"

Now it's up to the chief. His voice is clipped: "Flood fifty—hold it: flood one hundred!"

His gaze takes in the depth gauges and the water column in the Papenberg. "One hundred forward! And make it quick!"

Drops of perspiration splash rhythmically into the bilge which is gurgling softly beneath the floor plates. The periscope motor hums for a second. This indicates that the commander is only upping the periscope for an instant at a time and then letting the water close over it again.

Nothing but monotonous rudder orders coming down now, which are meaningless to all of us.

Suddenly the commander orders tube five to be flooded. I am totally confused: the stern tube?

I've lost track of the boat's movements. Could we possibly have made a one-hundred-and-eighty-degree turn?

The order is transmitted aft. Only seconds later the report comes back: "Tube five standing by for under-water firing when torpedo door opened." Two or three minutes go by.

"Connect tube five!"

The Papenberg indicates that the periscope is submerged. The sight of the sinking water column seems to affect the chief like a physical pain. He cringes and gives an order to the hydroplane operators. The periscope is clear again. I can feel the relief.

"Tube five standing by?" asks the commander.

"Jawohl, Herr Kaleunt!"

From time to time the chief corrects the hydroplane position: "Forward zero, aft ten down!"

The diesel stoker standing by and shutting off the external exhaust valves. Now the boat can dive, without any water getting into the engine through the diesel exhausts.

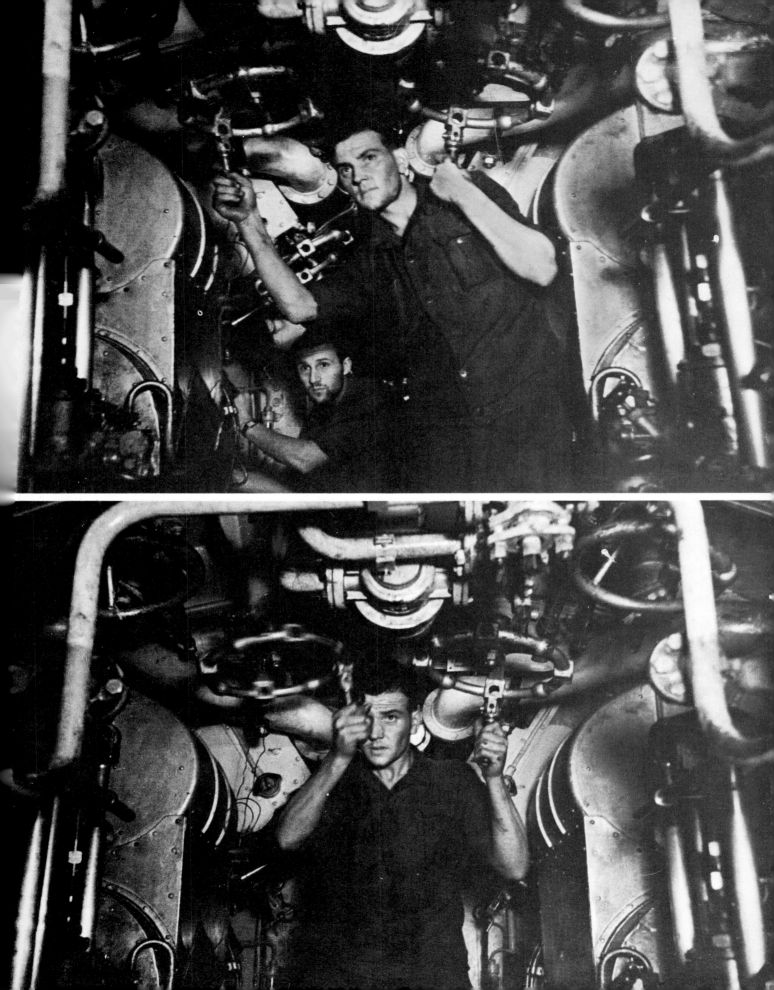

Our eyes no longer meet. We are hopelessly confused. There is nothing we can do other than stand there, both blind and deaf, in anticipation of the commander's orders.

The commander wants to know the position of the helm.

"Rudder fifteen degrees starboard!" is the immediate reply.

The tension is excruciating. The only sound to be heard is the brief hum and halt of the periscope motor—a sinister Morse language.

Then the commander's urgent voice from above: "All hands forward! Dive to two hundred feet! Fast!"

I hadn't expected anything so dramatic. What could have happened?

The men come rushing through the control room from astern. The boat becomes distinctly bow-heavy.

Amidst the scuffling and the dragging of feet, the commander's voice: "Depth charges on the way!" And now he comes clambering down and takes a seat atop the chart chest: his calm and collected look is very persuasive.

"Forward hard down!" says the chief. "Up astern!"

We are defenseless: at this depth we cannot make use of our weapons.

The first crashing sledgehammer blow causes everything to shudder. One man who wasn't holding onto anything staggers and almost falls. The second blow makes all the lights go out. White cones from flashlights cast circles into the darkness. Someone calls for new fuses.

Another explosion, as massive and precise as its predecessors. What about the buoyancy cells? Have they been blown already? I haven't taken in that particular order.

The sound of the drain pump springing into action mingles with the hissing of the water rushing back into the hole the bomb has torn in the sea.

The auxiliary lighting goes on.

"Forward up! Hold it!" says the chief to the hydroplane operators.

Then he reports to the commander: "Boat steady!"

Because the chief is standing in my way, I cannot see how deep we are.

The commander now has to keep on calculating all the time. The basic factors in his reckoning change with each report from the sound man at the hydrophone. The boat creeps slowly through the depths. Meanwhile, the destroyer can race up and down on the surface under full steam: a predatory poacher fishing with bombs.

The sound man keeps up a running report on the bearings: "Two hundred and sixty degrees—two hundred and fifty degrees—two hundred and forty degrees—getting louder!"

Still wearing their streaming wet rubber gear, two bridge guards have settled down in front of the hydroplane buttons. The gauge indicates that the boat is well on its way down.

"Hard a-port!" orders the commander and immediately thereafter: "To sound shack: We're turning to starboard!"

The shine of perspiration throws the faces into sharp relief.

We wait for the next lot of bombs—motionless, with bated breath.

Seconds stretch into eternities—nothing.

At last we hear from the sound man again: "Destroyer noise growing weaker!"

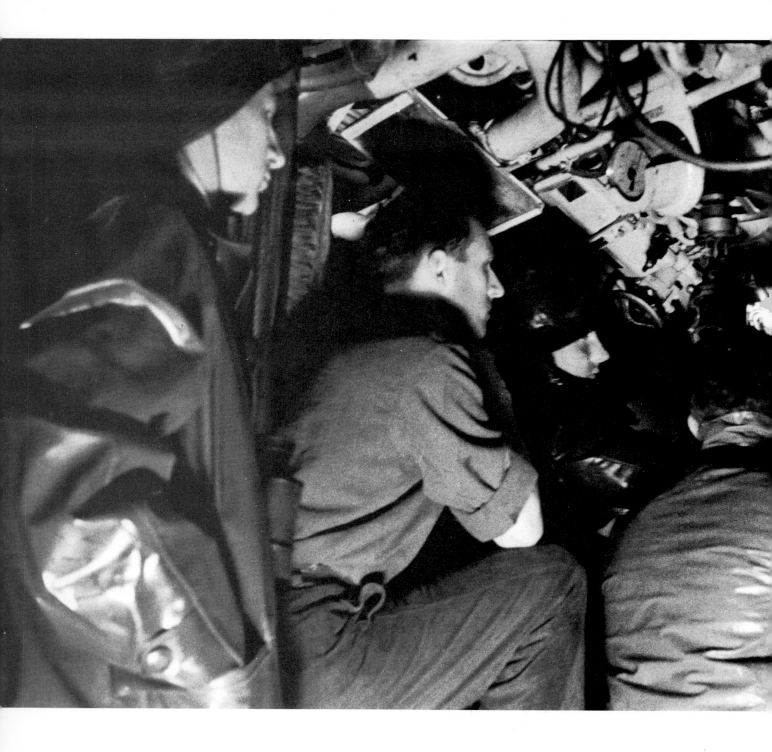

"Acknowledged!" says the commander. What is that supposed to mean?
Two more depth charges. But the sound of their explosions is significantly fainter.
The commander straightens up.
Another three, four charges—but even farther away.
The sound man is now slowly scanning the full circle of his scale.
"Well?" asks the commander, with a hint of mockery in his voice.
"Moving off!"
"Get me a piece of paper!" demands the commander. Is he really going to start drafting a radio message?
The chief, who's been on an inspection tour astern, returns to the control room.
He exchanges a glance with the commander: all in order.
The commander gives the order: "Go to periscope level!"
The chief gives his instructions. The commander climbs back into the tower.
And again the voice comes down from heaven: "Request depth."
"Forty-eight feet—periscope surfacing!"
The periscope motor hums quietly. Minutes go by. Not another word from above. The tension is getting unbearable.
Suddenly the commander's voice: "Crash dive! Deep!"
"All hands forward!" orders the chief.
But we just had that. Does every act have to have a repeat performance like something in a circus?
Again the boat grows bow-heavy. Again the needle on the depth gauges moves forward: twenty, thirty, forty—just as before, as though we could only understand it all the second time around.
The commander comes climbing down rung by rung into the control room— also exactly as before.
The commander takes his time. Eventually he says: "The destroyer is about three thousand feet away. Just parked there. Wanted to give us a surprise."
"He's right—from his point of view," I hear someone say next to me.
"Idiots," growls the commander.
The boat starts creeping away, frequently changing course. After a while, the commander starts grumbling: "We can't just keep on sitting down here in the cellar! The convoy will slip right through our hands!"
The chief tries his best to look concerned.
I ask the sound man to let me have his headset for a moment. The sound

In the control room during the destroyer's attack. The boat attempts a stealthy getaway under water. Only the sound man has any sensory perception now of the enemy's presence. But when he no longer has any bearing to report, the boat creeps on, changing course constantly. On his haunches behind the hydroplane operators, the chief keeps an eye on the depth gauge and the trim indicator.

close to my ear is like that of a huge seashell. But suddenly, that sounds like a propeller noise. There it goes again!

I hastily return the headset to the sound man. He listens keenly. Then he moves his lips: "Typical prowling. Hydrophone's revving!" He doesn't see fit to make a proper report. Perhaps because the commander is squatting right next to him in the passage.

"What's his bearing, then?"

"Two hundred and twenty degrees!"

The membranes of our hydrophone equipment on the flanks of our bow only give us rough bearings. Let's hope that the 220 degrees is accurate.

Nothing.

The chronometer is ticking away.

Now the commander moves over to the chart chest. I sit down next to him. The commander puts up his feet and stares moodily at the tips of his boots.

"Two hundred and seventy degrees. Moving slowly ahead . . . getting louder!"

"Great," says the commander. Then, more softly, to me: "I wouldn't bank on it."

"Two hundred and eighty degrees. Getting louder."

What fun, if this keeps up . . .

A whole hour must have ticked away before the sound man reports that he can no longer hear any noise. The commander has the boat taken to periscope depth again.

The eyes of the men beside him are all staring at his mouth. What will be his next order?

The commander is chewing on his lips the way he always does when he's thinking hard. He screws up his eyes and his forehead is furrowed. Suddenly his features relax and the command comes loud and clear: "Rig for surface!"

So he's decided to throw caution to the winds. He's determined to get his convoy back, come hell or high water!

With a hiss, the compressed air rushes into the diving cells. "Hatch clear!" reports the chief. The commander climbs up the ladder.

"Compensate pressure!"

The excess pressure is eliminated and the commander raises the tower hatch.

"Prepare to blow tanks!" The voice sounds as triumphant as a clarion call. I'm just thinking "Thank Christ," when the voice of command continues up above: "Stand by to vent—engine room stay rigged for diving!"

So we can't turn the page yet. The dance can start up again at any moment.

But after a while the commander does call for both diesels to be started up and the bow turned in what we assume to be the direction of the convoy. I take a deep breath.

Meanwhile it's turned dark up above. Which may be why the commander didn't even bother to take a look all the way around through his periscope. When it's dark and the weather is so bad, he can't expect to see much through the periscope anyway.

The second watch officer stands next to the control room mate, ready to return to the bridge. His watch is not yet over.

Surface Attack

I don't know which of the bridge guards mentioned it first. But suddenly we all agree: there's a smell of fuel oil in the air. The convoy battle must be in full swing over in that direction, from where the wind is blowing. The fumes of burning oil are its carrion stench.
The commander tests the wind and has our course adjusted.

In the dusk the starboard forward lookout discovers a strangely tinted cloud beneath the stratum overhanging the horizon. The commander is summoned to the bridge and contemplates the suspicious-looking apparition through his binoculars. After a few minutes of concentrated observation he gives the helmsman, standing in the tower directly below the bridge, the order to change course. The boat is racing with both diesels turning over at full speed toward the great dark mass. A cloud of smoke—no doubt of it. But as we approach it swells to more and more gigantic proportions—so gigantic that it can't be coming from an ordinary smokestack. There must be a ship—a tanker—on fire. Some boat must have torpedoed it. But why hasn't it sunk completely? It's a mystery.

Now we can see flames and the outline of a superstructure. A blast of wind presses the heavy black smoke down over us. Suddenly we are enveloped in stinking swathes of it. An urge to cough chokes my throat.

The war log gives the following account of what happened next:
17:42. Come to. Prepare for attack. Establish that vessel is smoking amidships.
18:55. Glare. A tanker. Running slow. 7 sea miles. Course approx. 120°. Surface attack feasible because coming through wall of smoke. On approach make out name: Arthur F. Corvin, London, 10,516 GRT. (The entry for 17:12 says that the *A. F. Corvin* was torpedoed. We search the area for the U-boat which must have torpedoed the steamer, but find nothing.)
19:50. Attack under way.

19:55. Bow torpedo at a distance of about 2,500 feet. Score a hit amidships.

The violence of the explosion churns the water into a huge white Christmas tree—twice as high as the steamer's masthead. The ship sags even farther into the water but stays afloat.

Where can the crew be? There seem to be some men standing astern. But that could well be an optical illusion.

The guns on the superstructure are clearly visible through the binoculars. Guns that are no longer manned.

Try as I may, I can see no lifeboats.

Our next torpedo hits the ship farther aft. But again the hit has scant effect. The steamer is still moving on. And yet the target is as easy as a clay pigeon. Distance some thirteen hundred feet.

Given such propitious circumstances, the commander is reluctant to fire another of the electric torpedoes sitting in their tubes. "We can do it more cheaply," he says. "We still have some of those bubbling torpedoes, don't we?"

In great haste one of the compressed air torpedoes is loaded. These can be treacherous because they generate a trail of bubbles and are easier than the electric ones to locate by hydrophone. They are fitted with a contact detonator.

This one hits the ship just to the back of the mizzen mast and flings up a geyser of horrendous beauty—of water, flames, and debris. At a height of about six hundred feet, the massive pillar spews out a fiery mushroom, which holds for seconds against the dark backcloth of the sky: the exploding cargo must have multiplied the torpedo's own charge many times over.

When the pillar does eventually collapse, pieces of wreckage come hurtling down with the mass of water. A sound of exploding cauldrons comes booming across to us.

But the carcass is still afloat. Tongues of red flame flicker along its entire length. They tint the belly of the monstrous maggot of smoke, now swelling to huge proportions out of the ship in place of the pillar; the smoke is sucked upward as though by a whirlwind.

Suddenly a fireworks display of pink and blood-red rockets breaks through the smokescreen and showers the surrounding sea right up to where we are with a flickering spray of red light. They must have gone off spontaneously. The mizzen mast sticks out like a warning finger from this inferno of fire and smoke.

"No need for a coup de grâce." The commander's voice is hoarse.

Yet, beneath its cloak of flames, the dark mass of the stern is visible still. It is the only part remaining above water and it is leaning toward us. From time to time I catch sight through the smoke of the slanting deck, part of the superstructure, the stump of a derrick—but not a single member of the crew. Where can they be?

All around the wreck, dark red flames rise straight off the water: the cargo of fuel is leaking. The antagonistic elements of water and fire combine. The sea is burning. Even the strongest swimmer meets with a ghastly end in such a hell—burned in the water, corroded by the oil, suffocated by the smoke, he dies a manifold death.

The boat has made straight for a cloud of dense black smoke. As we approach, it grows to such dimensions that it cannot be any ordinary cloud coming from a ship's funnel: it has to be a burning tanker. It must have fallen behind the convoy we've been looking for. The tanker's course is due east—perhaps it was bound for Ireland. The whole thing is rather mysterious.

A direct hit amidships. The explosion produces a high, oddly shaped pillar but otherwise has no effect. A second try and a second hit, just to the front of the quarter-deck. This time oil is spilled astern over the superstructure, which starts burning too.

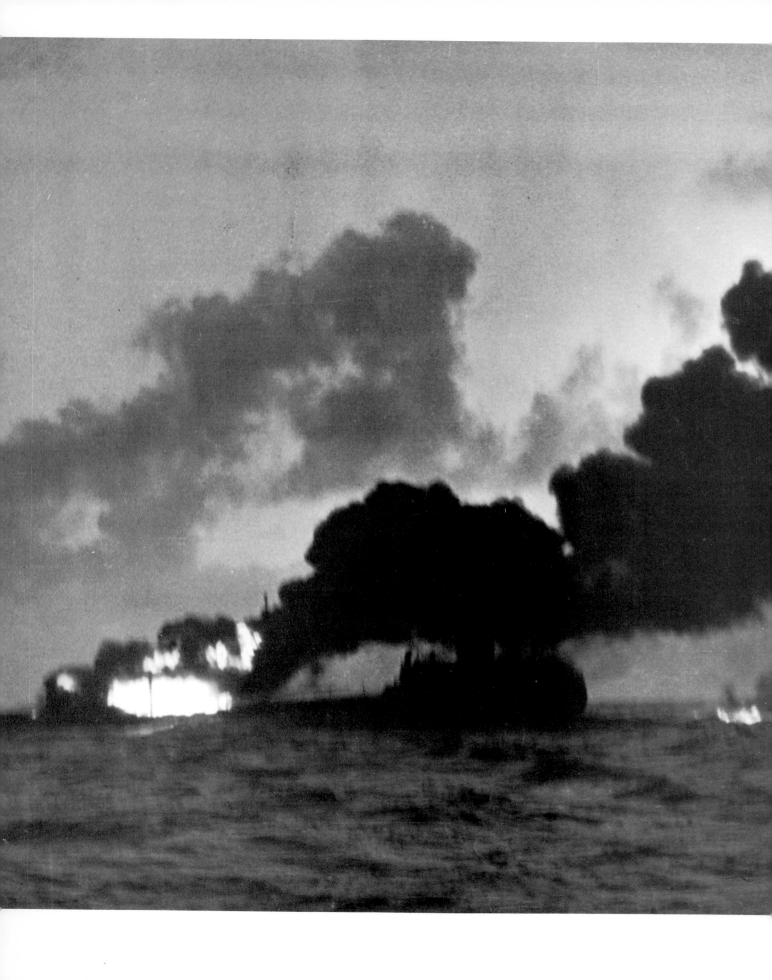

The ship is still not going down, though the fire is spreading. When a gust of wind lifts the cloud of smoke for an instant it seems to me that I can see human figures on the quarter-deck through my binoculars. A mass of spilled oil is now aflame directly on the water's surface.

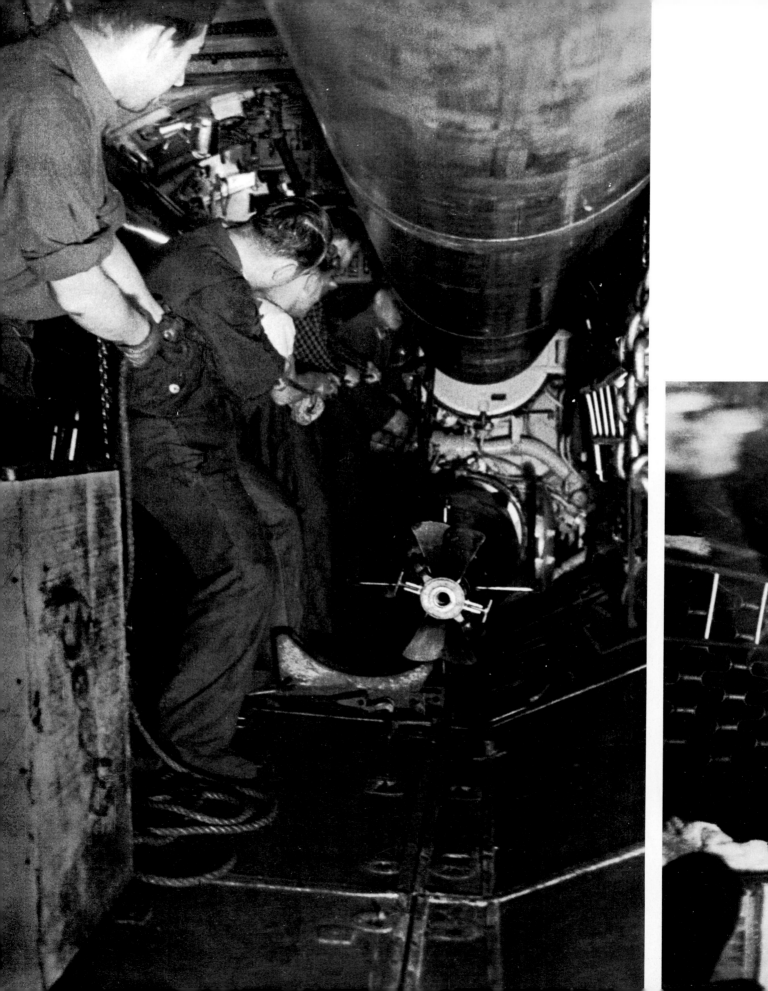

In the bow compartment during the attack; the lower starboard torpedo tube is reloaded—with one of the older types of torpedo that runs on compressed air. Because they leave a tell-tale trail of bubbles, their daytime use is to be avoided. Also they should not be used against convoys, because the escort vessels can locate them more easily than those propelled by electric motors. All those struggling with the horizontal hawser here in the confines of the bow compartment know that up above the commander is counting the minutes. Despite the heat, the men exert themselves to the point where their lungs are whistling.

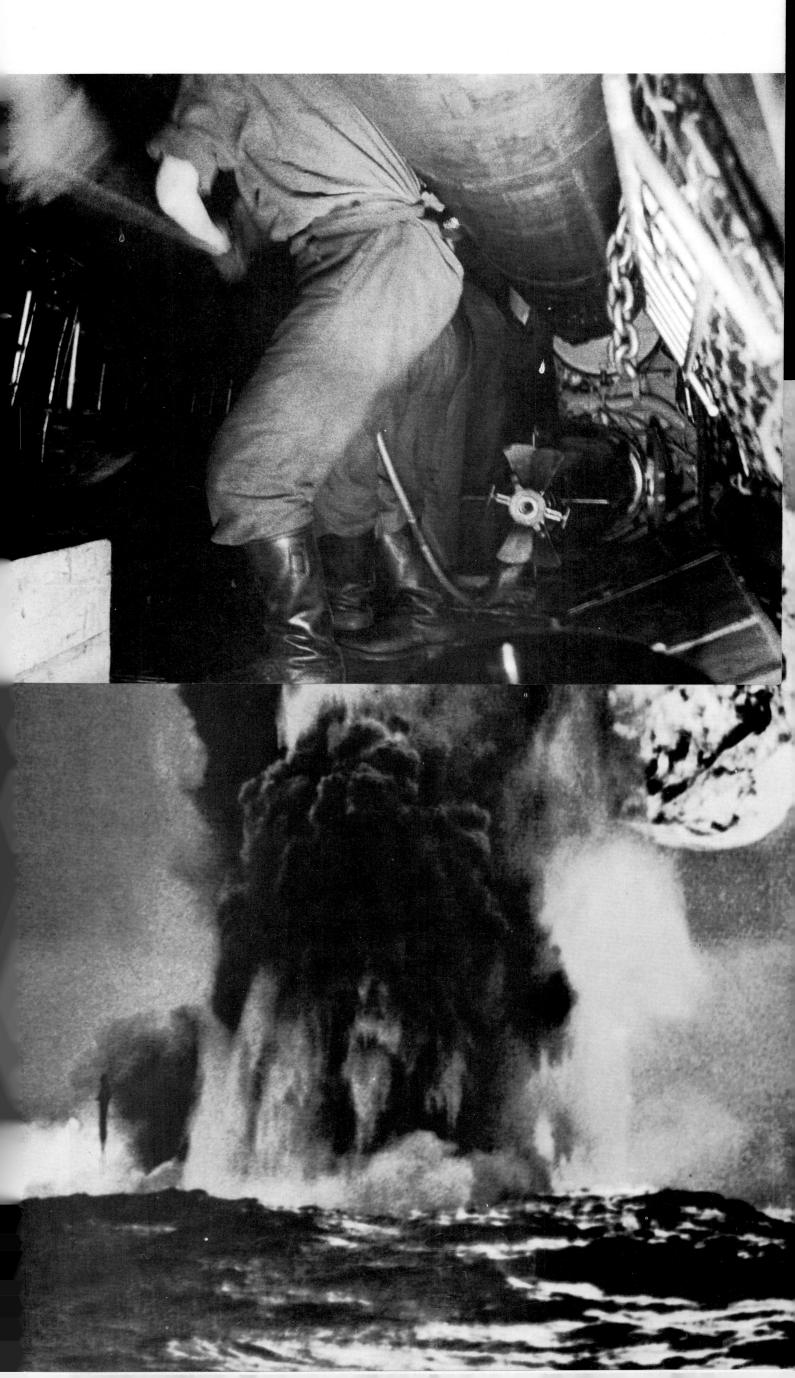

oddest angle to the room. It does me good to see that these sausages have something to say regarding our predicament. They tell me as much as any gauge about the trim of our boat. As I contemplate the sausage indicators, the first wave of terror subsides.

But then I hear the commander murmur: "It'll start again any moment."

Between the thumb and forefinger of my left hand I measure an imaginary sheet of steel: three quarters of an inch. That is all we have to preserve us from pressure of water and depth charge explosions.

A tremendous shock brings down my hand. A fearful ripping and crashing noise. And the trouncing continues, blow after blow.

The boat can't stand this for long. We're foundering! We're splitting at the seams! The green sea will come pouring in!

I have instinctively pulled my head down between my shoulders. When nothing happens, I venture a glance at the others: they're all standing hunched and rigid like pillars of salt.

A deprecatory wave of the commander's hand—he looks like a conductor letting his orchestra know that they've played badly.

Another blow. The water bursts apart as though it were a solid mass and the debris comes crashing down on the boat. Crockery smashes into pieces. The floor plates jump, clatter, and rock.

The pressure hull is being tested for stress resistance.

"They won't stop until they get into trouble!"

Who was that? Amateur theatricals out of sheer fright.

I have to pull myself together, do something. I do have my camera, after all. I clutch it and press the button when the floor starts dancing again.

It's sure to come out blurred. I've got no extra light, no flash. The exposure is far too long. The Tommies really could be more considerate. There'll be nothing much on the film. Nevertheless, I'll spend the last five shots on the commander.

Now I have to change the roll. In the process, I drop the lid of the camera and it skips away over the floor plates. This earns me a crushing look from the commander. I look pained, shrugging my shoulders: I'm simply not used to everything crashing around while I'm taking pictures, like in the innards of a drum.

In between one rudder order and another, the commander mutters, half to himself: "It can't possibly work." Is he referring to me or to the destroyer? "It all depends," I mutter back, just in case.

Once upon a time I was taught that if the film is underexposed you warm up the developer slightly. Gradually coax the faint negatives up to where they should be.

The commander gives no sign of having heard. He has to keep his mind on his calculations: our course—enemy course—evasive course. After a while he says softly: "There's more to come. They spotted the periscope!"

I notice that the chief's chin muscles are on the go again. They tighten and slacken rhythmically, as though he were doing exercises.

Four explosions in quick succession.

". . . fourteen . . . fifteen!" intones the control room mate. At every explosion, the depth gauge indicator goes right off the dial. No gauge is designed for this level of stress.

The commander in the control room. In accordance with the sound man's reports, he tries to maneuver the boat out of the path of the onrushing destroyer. Depth charges are exploding not far away. In due course it emerges that the commotion damaged the shutter on my camera.

Next double spread:
Inside the stern torpedo compartment during a renewed depth charge attack—the torpedo mechanic is standing by for orders next to the stern torpedo tube.

A quarter of an hour goes by like this. Then the commander gets to his feet and goes over to stand behind the helmsman, and pushes his hands into his pockets: That's that, is what he appears to be saying to indicate that he considers the matter closed.

The commander is staring ahead so fixedly that he looks totally withdrawn from his surroundings. In his imagination he's outside the boat. He is the only one fighting now. All our lives hang on his instinct and his decisions, on the speed of his reactions.

"Hard a-port!"

"Helm hard a-port!" comes the echo.

"Hold zero bearing!"

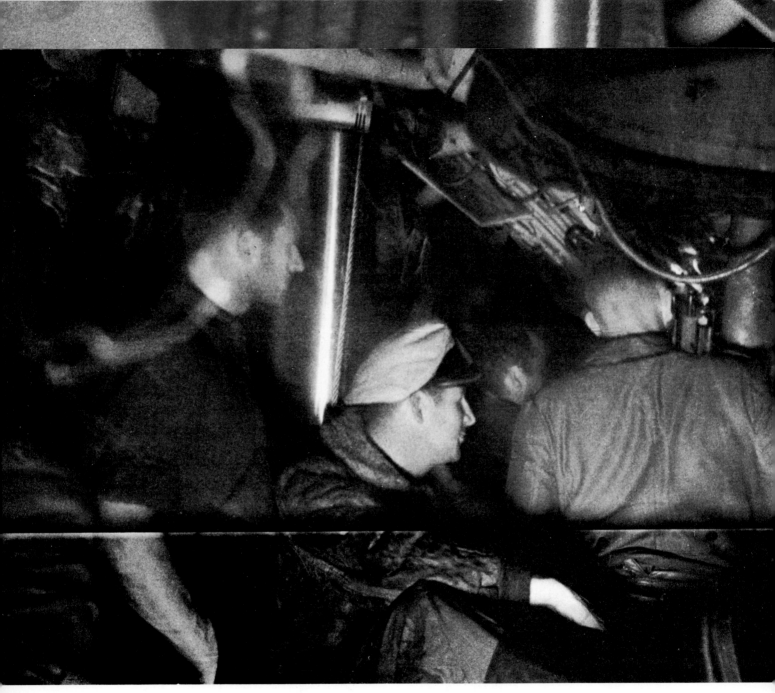

I get myself to the officers' mess and slump down on the leather sofa, the chief's bunk, absolutely exhausted. Suddenly I hear another round of depth charge explosions like distant thunder. My heart starts pounding instantly. I'm all ears, but can only hear the hum of our E-motors, as though from a great distance. Suddenly I feel all alone aboard. "No great adventure," I eventually hear someone say in the control room.

Suddenly I hear the chief fussing about the condensation and the dripping: "It's driving me nuts! There must be *something* we can do about it!"

We're still creeping along at a hundred and eighty feet with both E-motors going at one third.

The commander comes into the officers' mess grumbling: "Bloody shame we lost that convoy." As though he didn't know that our fuel reserves are exhausted anyhow.

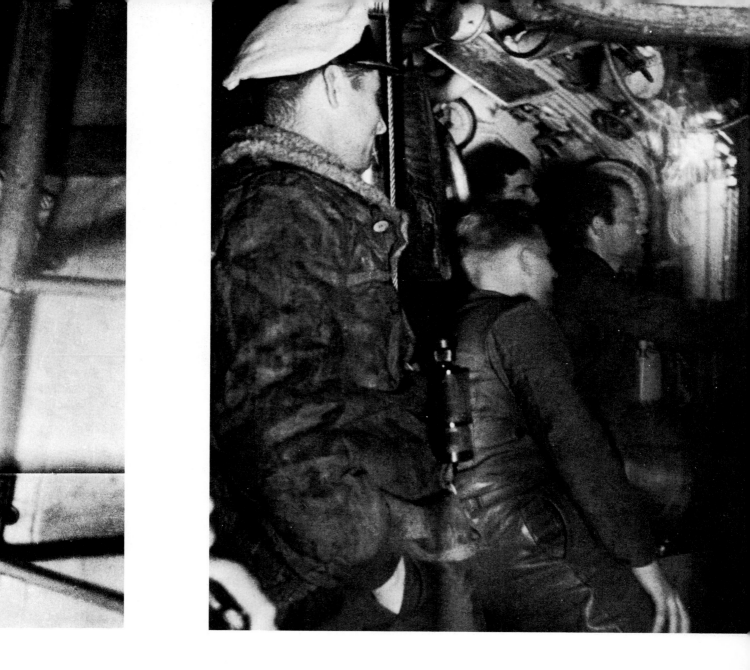

After another hour he orders us up to the surface. Even at this distance we can still see the reddish glare of the burning steamer; it looks like the night sky over a city. The men of the bridge watch are at their posts again, as usual, motionless behind their binoculars.

The commander has put his hands into his trouser pockets: for all those in the control room this signifies that the horror is over and we've come through.

After a while a report comes from below that radio messages have been received. The second watch officer makes his way down and returns before long with the news that U-456 has made contact with the convoy and already shot up one five-thousand-tonner.

"Then everything's shipshape, isn't it?" says the commander.

You've got to give him his due, I tell myself. He knows how to play it cool—and he always gets his effects.

Inside the engine room after the attack.
The chief mechanic and a diesel stoker inspecting the engines for possible damage. It seems that the camshaft of the starboard diesel has come to some harm. It cannot be the crankshaft—that's farther down. The chief engineer brings the plans along. He has even worse troubles to worry about: unidentified defects in several parts of the boat.

"Get me a piece of paper!" the commander demands a little later, as he is lying on his bunk. Is he planning to compose some artistic understatement for the war log? Or a report to Headquarters? Most likely he'll put down a mere: "Surprised by destroyer during rain squall—three hours of depth charge pursuit." I'd be amazed if he scribbled anything less laconic than that.

After a few minutes he turns up in the control room again. He exchanges a glance with the chief, then gives his order: "Go to periscope level!" and climbs unhurriedly up the rungs into the tower.
The chief has the hydroplanes adjusted. The commander's voice comes down to us: "Request depth!"
Everything is back to normal. In a minute we'll be cruising along through the night as a surface vessel, subject to the everlasting routine.

The commander has sought refuge behind his green curtain to write up the war log. He is a past master of this kind of writing and can spend days mulling over possible abbreviations of his text.

"13:00 begin return journey," is what the commander has written into the war log.

He now spends a lot of time on the bridge. Repeatedly he urges the bridge guards not to relax their concentration for a second. More than once the euphoria of knowing that they're homeward bound has cost crews their lives at the very last moment.

The chief wants to take my camera apart. The winding mechanism no longer works properly. Some fifteen minutes go by in speculations: what could one do to protect the camera against saltwater? Smother it all over, perhaps, in engine grease? Finally the chief goes and fetches his "special tools": delicate screwdrivers in a kind of spectacles case. He spreads a towel on the table and goes to work. My nerves are too frazzled to be able to sit and watch this display of the watchmaker's craft for long. I prefer to lie back on my bunk. But I can get no real rest: I keep trying to guess how many screws will be left over at the end of the operation. To make matters worse, the chief comes through the U-room and says: "First I have to make some proper tools: pincers and ultrafine screwdrivers. Don't worry, we'll get there!"

He fancies himself, I think to myself; that'll surely be the end of my camera.

Hours later, I go to the officers' mess to find the table already laid. I have to look twice: lying right in the middle, enthroned on a pile of plates, is my camera, polished within an inch of its life. "It's working," says the chief blandly, in his inimitable way, as though it was nothing to write home about.

The commander looks morose. I soon discover what's bugging him: before we meet up with our escort we probably won't get any air cover as we approach the coast.

"Christ, just look at us," he curses. "Whole fleets of enemy aircraft just to combat our few subs—and what do we have? Fuck-All! Atlantic Air Command: sounds terrific—except they don't have any planes!"

The mood aboard makes you think of homing pigeons: don't let them catch us now. We're getting closer to our own "western approaches." All the submarine routes converge in the vicinity of our bases. This is where the enemy lies in ambush, just the way we do close to the coastline of Britain.

There's a lot going on in the control room: lists are drawn up of things that need repairing and shipyard order forms are typed, along with lists of supplies we need from the stores, and furlough papers.

"Bureaucratic warfare," jokes the commander; the typewriter has taken root on the mess table.

When the danger is past and we're being escorted by a patrol boat with its

protective armament of mines and anti-aircraft batteries, the "subterraneans" are allowed up for a smoke and a chat in the "conservatory" on the afterdeck. Many have not had more than five minutes of fresh air throughout the voyage.

The coast is gradually getting larger. With all engines slow ahead we are making straight for the harbor channel. Soon we can almost smell dry land. The lines are being got ready on deck.

We act tough, suppressing any sign of excitement or anticipation. The elder of our two diesel mates says to me: "Leave—what does it amount to? Just putting off the evil day."

In a few minutes' time, the boat will tie up at the lock. The gangplank will be pushed across. Let's hope the mailbag follows without delay.

Close to the harbor mouth the sea is as flat as a pancake. Clouds of smoke coming from a tanker that has just arrived hide the jetty from our view. Our patrol boat is also puffing more smoke. Its wake glistens.

The men are already gathering on deck, seamen in front and off-duty engine crews behind.

The commander takes personal charge of the mooring maneuver. The bosun hurries the men along: "Come on—shift those lines!"

The officers are standing at attention. The commander returns the salute with a surly expression. What's eating him now?

At last the boat is made fast by the bow. The bowline and the spring are made fast. Then the sternline and sternspring. The first watch officer blows his whistle twice, sharply: "Get moving."

The commander calls down into the control room: "Boat moored! Stop engines! Reception on deck!"

"There used to be music," I hear someone say beside me.

The first watch officer and the chief engineer report to the commander: "First division standing by for inspection!"—"Engine crews and technicians standing by for inspection!"

The commander goes through the motions of inspecting his men. Then he steps back as far as he can on the narrow deck and calls: "Attention! . . . Eyes right!"

The Flotilla Commander staggers across the catwalk and comes climbing down the metal rungs on the side of the tower.

The commander laconically goes through the ritual: "Respectfully report U-ninety-six back from its mission to the front!"

The handshake is followed by all the other familiar routines.

"What on earth is that collection?" asks the second watch officer, astonished by the crowd on the pier. I take a closer look myself: those fur-coated ladies are not the usual carbolic dolls. And the men—can they be the Todt Organization? Or railway executives? And who's that, smirking at the back? Looks like the S.S. or the secret police. And what's that fellow doing here with his expensive trilby?

The naval representatives are pretty peculiar too—one of them is wearing gloves and carrying an Arriflex.

The commander's face is expressionless, his gaze like ice: these are not the kind of people he expected for our reception committee.

Typical Bay of Biscay weather. On the last leg of our journey to a "safe" home base, the men of the watch have to be particularly vigilant. The Royal Air Force concentrates its patrols on the submarine approaches to the Atlantic bases.

The signaler conveys a message to the patrol boat which has come to meet us and give us cover on our way in. The chief has come up from his realm of machinery and hoists the victory pennants. This custom, of hoisting a pennant for every steamer sunk, was introduced by Lieutenant Commander Arnaud de la Perière, World War I ace of aces. On one occasion he hoisted twenty-three. We have just two.

Every bit of damage the boat has suffered during its tough and lengthy voyage—be it the result of wear and tear or of depth charges—is carefully recorded as soon as it is discovered, down to the smallest worn-out bolt in the engines or broken hinge on a locker. The chief will arrange with members of the shipyard's Board of Works and representatives of the various workshops in what sequence the repairs will be done, when the boat should go into dock and when it should be ready to leave. The very thought of the harassment that has become the order of the day is enough to get people's backs up: they won't let us have a single day more leave than is absolutely necessary. Even while the boat is at the yard, a part of the crew has to remain on board to stand guard and to be there when the boat is transferred from its pen to one or another of the docks.

Confrontation upon arrival. Above, those standing on the pier: fur coats, tailored suits, gloves, smart uniforms, well-pressed breeches, and below, on the grating: us in our submarine gear, every bit as shabby as our boat.

It became obvious early on that the tide was turning in the submarine war. Way back in March of 1941, U-47 (Prien), U-99 (Kretschmer), and U-100 (Schepke) were lost to two different convoys. Only Kretschmer survived and was taken prisoner by the British. In December, U-567 (Endrass) was sunk by the depth charges of the British corvette *Samphire*.

So many highly decorated aces coming to grief one after the other spread great alarm and raised the life expectancy of their comrades: these latter were promoted to flotilla commanders, transformed into instructors, or detailed to the staff. Those who added oak leaves to their Knight's Cross now had to do without the swords, while those who had already been awarded swords had to dispense with the diamonds. They complained and even protested in an undertone about being withdrawn from the fighting, as we expected of them. But a more honest reaction was: "Let the young dogs show what they're made of."

The youngsters were made of lesser stuff than their elders. How could it be otherwise? While the first issue of commanders had had a peacetime merchant marine background or had served time in the Navy, which endowed them with a priceless store of experience, the newcomers were recruited from the ranks of ex-schoolboys and the Hitler Youth. Instead of being given careful training to make them at home out at sea, they were hustled through courses like eggs in an incubator. Besides, they'd had a harder time of it than their elders, who never had to combat highly sophisticated defenses. The days of "rabbit shooting" were well and truly over.

The younger men's attitude was: "If the old windbags had to do it right now, they'd never blast the hundred thousand tons out of these convoys you need for a Knight's Cross!"

A number of the young commanders—toward the end of the war the minimum age for a commander was lowered to twenty-one, that for chief engineers to twenty—lost their boats immediately en route from the German shipyards, up around Scotland, to the bases on the west coast of France. The RAF was in all but total control of these sea routes.

After the wash-out off the U.S. coast in 1942, the Submarine Division re-

Running on E-motors, the boat makes its way through the brackish water of the harbor toward its pen in the bunker. The victory pennants have already come down. The boat is berthed in one of the pens which can be drained and used as dry docks.

verted to their earlier wolf pack tactics, but the celebrated raids on convoys soon ceased to be as successful. Within a year the Allies had managed to improve their weaponry and tactics so markedly that the submarine war was to all intents and purposes lost. Nonetheless, broadcasts and newspapers continued boasting of triumphs with a medley of new figures—figures that were meaningless: one hundred thousand gross registered tons—one million gross registered tons. . . . The war turned into an accountant's plaything, an unreal balance sheet: so and so many ships are being built by the enemy, so and so many are sunk, so and so many still remain to be sunk for the books to be balanced. Our own rapidly increasing losses were not disclosed. The causes of so sudden an increase remained a mystery for quite some time. The High Command was groping in the dark, accepted the existence of radar, and believed at the same time that the short signals transmitted by boats maintaining contact with or attacking a convoy could not possibly be intercepted. The boats went on signaling, which brought many to their doom, since the Allies had developed the High Frequency Direction Finder, commonly known as Huff Duff (HFDF), which enabled them to intercept even the briefest radio signals with ease. The boats were located with precision, attacked, forced under water, or destroyed.

The story of convoy SC-118 was typical of the new situation: The submarine U-187 made contact and was destroyed immediately after it had reported the sighting by radio signal. Of the twenty-one boats flung against this convoy, only five even fired a shot throughout the four-day operation. They sank thirteen of the convoy's sixty-one vessels. This success exacted a high price: three boats were lost, four others turned back to base severely damaged.

Soon the cost of success rose even higher: in May 1943, forty-one German submarines went to the bottom of the sea.

The technical divisions of the Naval High Command had been caught napping. Neither in the field of electronics nor in that of weaponry did they keep pace with developments or even make any significant progress at all. Instead of investing in research and risking the necessary experimentation in good time, they concentrated on producing large numbers of one type of fighting vessel which, though proven in battle, was so conventional that it was almost indistinguishable from those of World War I. The truly revolutionary models with increased under-water speed and a greater diving capacity were completed far too late.

Dönitz ordered the boats back from the North Atlantic, kept talking of a lean period and promised new and better weapons—even phenomenal innovations. But in reality there was nothing going on—they just kept fiddling around. The submarine war continued, with inadequate means against strengthened defenses in the form of escort vessels (escort groups, support groups) and escort aircraft carriers, whose planes—together with land-based ones—controlled every square mile of ocean in the North Atlantic. These airplanes equipped with radar became the submarine's most dangerous adversaries.

In the early days it had all been much easier. A boat could move alongside a convoy, just out of sight: the steamers sent their clouds of smoke way up into

All the houses in the vicinity of the submarine base of St.-Nazaire have been bombed to rubble. The boats arrive and depart against a backdrop of ruins and empty window-sockets. The submarine war has entered its final phase of desperation. In days gone by, the mate with his arm in a sling would have been kept back in the hospital.

the sky despite the engineers, who did their utmost to minimize the fumes. They could be seen by the bridge watch of the submarine, which meanwhile remained hidden below the horizon. The mastheads of a destroyer, too, could be made out from a U-boat tower well before that same boat could be spotted by the man up in the destroyer's crow's nest—and even the lookout aboard an aircraft could not make out a submarine against the moving backcloth of the sea as easily as the bridge watch could see the plane against the sky.

But suddenly everything changed: wherever you turned there was radar. Radar on destroyers—radar in the air—even on steamers. The sound man's reports from the hydrophones turned into an endless litany: bearing faint, bearing getting louder . . . then the "uiuiui" going through the entire boat. And as soon as the sound man reported "Bearing stationary!" there was the inevitable alarm and the nerve-racking shrilling of bells. ·

It ceased to be possible for a lone boat to maintain contact, so boats had to take turns, and these were the rules of the game: dive—search—pursue—dive to escape aircraft—pursuit by hunter groups—depth charge attacks—and that was that: once you were down there, you lost all track of the convoy.

How much more difficult it became in time to get close to the convoys and how much wishful thinking was entered as real success on the balance sheet is clearly shown by the example of convoy RA-59: five boats were supposed to tackle this convoy in the North Sea during April and May of 1944. But only one of these boats—U-711—managed to sink a steamer of 7,176 gross registered tons. Three boats (U-277, U-674, U-959) were destroyed. One boat (U-307) hoisted four pennants, one for each victim, as it sailed into port. In due course it emerged that not one of the steamers or destroyers it had torpedoed had actually been sunk.

When circumstances made close observation of what was going on in a convoy difficult, many commanders were tempted into deceiving themselves. Headquarters, being remote, should have been more skeptical and examined claims more closely—but self-deception had meanwhile become a habit and the tally a deliberate fraud.

The aura of success had vanished. The gray whales were sent off without any fanfare: no music, no pretty nurses, and hardly any expectation of a safe return. The Submarine Division was at a loss. Its strategic and operational experiments became increasingly haphazard. Nothing was working any more. But despite all this, many crew members still believed that the promise of Final Victory from the lips of their Commander in Chief would yet be fulfilled.

Hardly any units of the German armed forces can have had more blind faith in their commander than the submarine units had in Dönitz.

For a long time, I myself thought of Dönitz as a kind of seafaring Moltke, until the time—even before he was appointed Commander in Chief of the Navy—when he revealed himself as a demagogue and indeed a blind fanatic; this characterization was confirmed, finally, with his ordinance of March 27, 1944, addressed to what he was pleased to call "the Invasion Boats," which sent submarine upon submarine, crew upon crew, to a certain death; such a strategy was long since rendered pointless in terms of the general war and made no less dreadful by being termed a glorious sacrifice.

The ordinance closed with the following words:

"Every commander must realize that at such a time [an enemy landing] the future of our German people depends more than ever before on him individually, and I demand of every commander that he disregard all otherwise applicable precautions and keep but a single goal fixed in his heart and mind: Attack—engage—sink!

"I know that I can rely on my U-boat men, tempered in the heat of battle, to carry out these instructions to the letter."

Since individual commanders chose not to understand the meaning of this ordinance, it was followed on April 1 by supplementary instructions:

"Every enemy vessel involved in an invasion, whether it carries a mere handful of soldiers or a single tank, is a target that demands an all-out submarine attack. It must be tackled even if there is danger of loss to ourselves.

"When it is a matter of striking at the enemy's invasion fleet, there can be no consideration of the possible threat of shallow water, of the conceivable presence of mine fields, no hesitation whatsoever.

"Every enemy soldier and weapon destroyed prior to an invasion diminishes that enemy's prospects for success.

"The boat that inflicts losses on the enemy at a time of invasion has accomplished its loftiest mission and justified its existence, even if it perishes in the process."

Until that time, despite the horrors of war, certain principles still counted for something: that a ship and its crew, the sailors, did matter, and that even in wartime the relationship between means and ends had to obey some economic rationale.

Had the argument put forward by the Admiral to justify his command been sound—namely, that many more land troops than the crew of a submarine, and quantities of equipment and arms, would be needed to destroy the arms and soldiers of a barge once it landed, and therefore sacrificing a boat was worthwhile—it would by analogy have been reasonable to sacrifice a company of soldiers to the capture of a few boxes of ammunition, on the grounds that the boxes contained five thousand rounds capable of killing five thousand men, many more than those of a single company.

This example illustrates the technique of apparent logic intended to give blind fanaticism a veneer of military rationality. The frivolous slogan "Tie down their forces," which is still trotted out to this day, tried to give some meaning to meaningless last-ditch fighting and to justify senseless sacrifice. It bears witness to the same kind of mentality.

Already on June 8, 1943, the war log of the Naval High Command had this to say:

"The current crisis, a crisis of development in armaments, can and must be weathered. Should it transpire even then that the successes of our submarines cannot be augmented to the point where they prove fatal to the enemy, the submarine war will nonetheless be a defensive value to be retained, because the battle of the Atlantic ties down vast enemy forces, which would become available to the enemy for an assault on Europe if the submarine war were halted."

(To call the submarine war "a value to be retained" strikes one—who can not ever shrug off the vision of its victims—as particularly shabby.)

If it could score no great "successes," the deployment of submarines was at

The Thinning of the Ranks

One boat has returned to base. The commander takes a hasty shave. Duly improved by spit and polish, he appears before the Flotilla Commander to submit his war log and the record of the sea routes he has traveled.

The commander feels nervous and insecure. It is always the same: the change is too sudden. Nobody coming in from the cold like that can adjust so rapidly. For the first few days, they all feel rather like uninvited guests, whose unexpected presence is an embarrassment. The Flotilla Commander tries to put the returning wanderer at his ease by refraining from asking questions. The conversation is one between experts.

Our skipper is almost apologetic about his feats: "I had no choice . . ." "It was peculiar . . ."

His superior takes care not to make him feel awkward: no praise, no word of admiration for the hard-won successes. We all try to behave as though this were an ordinary morning meeting. But perhaps that in itself is a mistake. The commander is bound to notice that we're just acting casual and behaving as if on cue, treating him like a madman who has to be spoken to as the complete opposite, so that he won't notice.

The commander seems unaware of his Flotilla Chief's searching glances: our commander is one of the youngest. A narrow, emaciated face with huge eyes. From time to time he shakes his head almost imperceptibly, as though trying to rid himself of some kind of physical irritation. His sudden lapses into silence, excessively prolonged silence, make an odd impression.

None of us can bring ourselves to say anything. If only the Flotilla Chief would make some funny remark which would give us a chance to laugh. If only he would say something that would crack a smile, take us out of our misery.

Eventually the commander does get going and starts telling his story: "Alarms all day long. Just on and on. They were as stubborn as terriers. A few depth charges more or less—so what? What did they care? We got to the point when we were actually pleased to hear them dropping whole carpets on us—we told ourselves they'd run out of bombs more quickly that way. But the

When the ships of a submarine hunter-killer group appear on the scene, a boat is obliged to dive. That is the sign the aircraft have been waiting for: like hawks they streak down to bomb the boat just as it's diving, when it is totally defenseless. The time span required for diving is practically the same as that of the air approach (some forty seconds). But before the boat can make its getaway under water, the exhaust vents of the diving cells must be left open. An explosion needs to have only a minimal effect on something, on these vents for example. The damage it wreaks produces a chain reaction. The boat goes out of control. Many submarines have gone to the bottom that way on their very first mission.

Five boats are moored simultaneously in the lock. That has never happened before. Gangplanks are thrown out to link the decks. Now the Flotilla Commander can promenade from boat to boat. On each of them he calls the crew together. There is nothing much he can tell them. Everyone knows only too well what lies ahead: the boats will leave in a bunch to make sure that they'll

These boats are equipped with a remodeled tower and a second "conservatory." They now have a 37-mm. cannon on the aft platform, along with two sets of 20-mm. twins on the conservatory proper.
The outline of the bridge has been modified too, by the addition of a Metox mattress. The boats are now deployed in groups, so as to have more firepower in case of attack by the Royal Air Force.

get away at all. Our newest trick: concentrated anti-aircraft defenses.

This time there is no festive sendoff, no girls with flowers, no shipyard workers, no Todt Organization fat cats, no soldiers. Since there is no band on the pier, a mate aboard the second boat gets out his accordion and one crew after the other joins in the singing:

"... we've barely been a day on shore
before the Ocean calls once more."

"This time the cap really fits!" I hear one of the seamen next to me say scornfully. The great draw-bridge goes up yet again: a sixth boat is coming into the lock. The draw-bridge goes down again and a detachment of infantry comes marching noisily across the planks. The crews wave to the steel-helmeted soldiers. The soldiers wave back. Soon the water begins to swirl under the stern of the first boat, the outer sluice-gate opens and slowly each boat parts a little from the others. Which of them will return? The chances are three to one against. At best, only two of these water-borne gladiators will make it back. Which are they? Which are the others?

The Demise of the Atlantic Bases

After their breakthrough at the vertex of the angle formed by the peninsula of Cotentin and the westward salient of Brittany, the Allies advanced their tanks in a southwesterly direction in order to isolate the German naval bases on the Atlantic coast. They quickly succeeded in cutting off the harbors of Brest, Lorient, and St.-Nazaire. A cordon of destroyers and patrol boats barred the exits to the sea. From the Allied point of view, that was sufficient for the time being. For the Germans it meant being under siege.

Though one Atlantic base after another was encircled by the Allies and the defeat of the submarines a foregone conclusion, Dönitz saw fit to dictate the following entry into the war log on August 26, 1944: "The submarine war will continue in the same spirit and with new means."

I find myself amongst those confined to Brest by the Sixth U.S. Armored Division.
There can be no doubt that the harbor of Brest and its wide and sheltered roads would be very valuable to the U.S. Navy and that prolonged resistance is out of the question. We therefore have to reckon with the speedy capture of Brest.
For the two submarine flotillas based at Brest, keeping the boats out of enemy hands has become the main objective. This means that they must somehow be repaired and made fit to return to battle, or else they must at least be patched up to enable them to dive and cruise and thus attempt the risky transfer to bases farther south. Several units are formed for the defense of the immediate base area with men of the personnel reserve and the staff of the base administration, and all those remaining are handed over to the fortress commander, to be integrated by him into the battle-scarred rump units charged with the defense of the perimeter. The backbone of the defense is the Second Paratroop Division, whose retreat toward us has been severely

hampered by street barricades along the way and by mines planted by the Resistance. What the soldiers have to tell convinces us that it is now impossible to get out of Brest by the overland route.

Much fuss is made about the shortage of snorkels. There are two boats without them down in the shelter. Some snorkels are supposedly on their way here by road on huge tractor trailers. Nobody believes that they might still get through. Then, late one evening, a truck does turn up after all. Both the driver and the co-driver are released French prisoners of war. How they managed to get to us remains their secret. They must have fed the Maquis a real story. The flotilla, needless to say, affords them a princely welcome.

Our numbers are swelled by small artillery units without guns and infantry from Coastal defense—plus local troops retreating to the fortress from the surrounding countryside. There are no more planes. The North Brest squadron, which occasionally gave the U-boats air cover, has been withdrawn.

Operations rooms are installed in two large shelters located on the base. Defensive positions are built at several outposts, complete with shrapnel shields, trenches, and machine-gun emplacements. One semi-automatic submarine flak gun is positioned next to the main entrance, outside the wall and aimed at the approach road.

Not that this will enable us to put up any great resistance against a well-equipped opponent. We simply mean not to be overrun. Besides, the whole business allows us a hedge against sabotage.

The Flotilla Commander and the commander of the harbor installations are arguing furiously: they have received orders to destroy the harbor completely before it is captured. The port commander has laid careful plans to ensure that ships will be sunk at their moorings and that all wharfs and hangars will be blown up. Since the capabilities for reconnaissance on land or sea are zero and since one cannot disregard the possibility that the Americans might suddenly break through our feeble defenses, the port commander worries that he may not get the chance to stage his grand destruction. Wanting to save his skin, he's anxious to set off the explosives right now. But the submarines still need a gap to make their getaway. This gives rise to stormy discussions about buying time. Eventually ships are sunk between the pier-heads in such a manner that the submarines can just inch their way through.

Surprisingly enough, the French Underground doesn't stir: nothing in the way of Maquis activity in Brest.

A truce is negotiated with the Americans to give the French population time to evacuate the city.

The Americans call upon General Ramcke, commander of the paratroopers, to surrender, but he refuses to do so.

In the final struggle for the fortress of Brest, the naval units suffer severe casualties, for they were never trained to fight on land. I do not witness this final struggle myself; I have been ordered on board what will be the last German submarine to abandon the base.

Standing at the very tip of our bow, the bosun tries to get a line to the swimmers. Among the men in the rubber dinghies, some are severely injured. The liferaft carries a huddle of men who are totally exhausted.

went into the water. Their first watch officer is wearing his cap. He kept it on _____ *The control room mate, who*

enemy vigilance.

The reckless even turn sarcastic: "That must mean that we can expect them to get here any minute." Or: "They'll be the Flying Dutchmen—ships with no harbor to go to."

They seem to have forgotten the famous decree issued by Dönitz—"To Combat Smear Campaigns and Petty Complaints"—on September 9, 1943, which contained the following:

"Those who openly transmit their own miserable attitudes to their comrades or to other fellow-Germans and thereby paralyze the will to persist in armed self-assertion are to be held rigorously responsible by summary tribunal for corroding the Armed Forces.

"With the national-socialist worldview, the Führer has laid the foundation for the unity of the German people. It is the task of each and every one, in the present phase of the war, to safeguard this precious unity with rigor, patience, and steadfastness, through our struggle, our work, and our silence."

When one commander plucks up the courage to ask the Regional Commander of Submarines how he expects the miracle boats to be finished at all, given that the shipyards are being constantly bombarded, he is told: "Don't worry about it and don't bother your superiors! Ever since the Führer entrusted the submarine building program to Reichsminister Speer everything has been moving along just fine. Faith in the Führer is a German officer's first and foremost duty."

The men now parody the chorus of that hoary battle song: "The Rotten Bones Are Quaking":

> "We'll go on marching, marching, marching,
> Though the shit rains from on high
> We're heading back to mudville—
> Bergen's the arsehole in the sky."

The buck-passing starts in earnest even before the surrender: on March 3, the "Admiral for special duty" attached to the Commander in Chief of the Navy, notes:

"The Führer and the C-in-C of the Navy discuss at length and in detail the question of whether the Navy was built up appropriately prior to the war. The C-in-C of the Navy maintains that it was a mistake not to build much greater numbers of submarines rather than battleships, since we could never hope to make good the advantage our enemies held in the construction of battleships, while a superior submarine force would have had a considerable chance of deciding the war rapidly in our favor."

Even nowadays, you can read things like this: "If Dönitz had had approximately one hundred submarines at this time [in 1940], the destruction of shipping would have sapped Britain's vital energy."

But he didn't have them. In the early summer of 1940 there were precisely nineteen boats in the Atlantic.

But even supposing he had had more . . . A world war like this one could not be decided one way or another in a single theater of operations like the Atlantic. This particular war was lost from the outset.

What a difference between this picture and earlier ones. There used to be a guard of honor, a military band, a troop inspection. . . . Now there is a Flotilla Commander standing all alone in the midst of broken crates and barrels, with the pier looking like the outskirts of a wholesale market. His own score lists 24 vessels totaling 174,326 gross registered tons. This herd of steamers was sunk by him on three different boats in the course of eight missions. Dönitz fixed the Knight's Cross around his neck. The oak leaves he received from the Führer in person. Now he stands on the side of the pier, hunched in his leather coat—at thirty-four he is one of the oldest—and watches one of his very last boats drift in on E-motors, without any victory pennants fluttering from its periscope, to be handed over to the enemy.

The final words of the last report by the Western High Command, which issued from the Headquarters of the Admiral of the Fleet on May 9, 1945,

routes, in the hope that some vessel would pass at the exact angle that would accommodate the submarine's torpedo. The likelihood of this happening more than once in a while was remote, all the more so because the British had meanwhile refined the system of pinpointing submerged submarines with sonar. A submarine abiding by the rules of warfare at sea thus had only a slim chance of ever troubling either merchantmen or warships. It was not surprising, then, that the German shipbuilding program treated the submarine in a niggardly fashion prior to the outbreak of the war in 1939. In some years, no submarines were built at all. In other years there were merely a few experiments. It was only after the passage of time and many laborious debates that the most important submarine types were put into production. Those in charge thought of the submarine as a negligible factor. They were more inclined to build battleships, heavy cruisers, destroyers, even aircraft carriers, a "regular fleet," as it was called: harmoniously balanced, impressive to look at and "compatible"—easily integrated into an alliance.

The submarine met none of these requirements. And yet, when war broke out, "five years too soon"—as the Chief of the German Navy put it with a measure of resignation on September 3, 1939—the submarine was the Navy's only hope.

One man knew that from the first. With verve and passion, with pressing appeals to the leadership of the Navy and the state, he sought to propagate his view that the submarine was Germany's most incisive and most promising weapon in the war against England: Karl Dönitz, the Commander in Chief of Submarines.

His name is so intertwined with the history of the submarine war that one could almost speak of a dialectical interrelationship between him and "his" boats. No other military leader or commander was ever identified so fully with a particular weapons system as Dönitz was with the submarine war in general.

There were good reasons for this. Initially, when Dönitz was entrusted by Raeder in 1935 with the development of the submarine force, the ambitious captain feared that his military career was being maneuvered onto a siding, and Raeder, who never liked Dönitz, wouldn't have minded if that had been the case. But within a few weeks, the Commodore came to realize what an opportunity he had been given. Contrary to conventional wisdom, which held the submarine to be a subsidiary weapon, he believed it was the key to military success against England. He was quick to appreciate that it was in Britain's and not at all in Germany's interest to denigrate the submarine. If a war at sea was a struggle for control of the sea, then the Germans were playing a losing game—hadn't even the gigantic efforts of Emperor Wilhelm II and Tirpitz come to a humiliating end off Scapa Flow? Nothing was to be gained by ranged naval battles in the North Sea and the Atlantic. British supremacy on the Atlantic could never be broken, but it could quite literally be subverted—by the submarine.

For the submarines did not join battle with the enemy's warships; their real targets were enemy freighters. Control of the seas was nothing other than the ability to guarantee one's own merchantmen a safe passage, while curbing the enemy's ability to do likewise. Since there was no gainsaying that the

British blockade was effective, the Germans had to recognize early on that they couldn't maintain their own Atlantic trade routes. There was nothing for the German Navy to protect in the Atlantic. Therefore, the German High Command had only one single aim: the destruction—despite British sea power—of the objects of that power's protection; namely, the essential life-lines of Britain's overseas trade. No surface vessels were needed for this objective; submarines were sufficient; indeed, they were uniquely qualified for the job, since they could make themselves invisible and hide from the regular British fleet.

Dönitz drew the obvious conclusion: if Britain was the target, then Germany had to build submarines, and the more the better, since their technical and tactical characteristics demanded that they be deployed in large numbers. Dönitz was fully persuaded by the experience of 1918 that a mere handful of submarines could inflict no more than pinpricks on the British merchant marine: the likelihood of finding enemy vessels was always slight, because reconnaissance was not the submarine's forte. A single submarine could patrol no more than a limited stretch of the Atlantic and carried only a restricted number of torpedoes. When these were spent, the boat was useless—like a certain U-556, which had to look on helplessly as the *Bismarck* was hounded to its death, because it was "spent."

For quite some time, Dönitz's plea for more submarines went unheeded in the offices of the High Command. Anger and bitterness built up within him: he knew what ought to be done, but the leadership of the Navy and the state would not listen. Raeder took Hitler's assurances to heart, that there would never be a war with England, that things would never get that far, and he therefore planned one "regular fleet" after another, each one bigger and more splendid than the last. He wanted Germany's naval forces to be beautiful: with many beautiful battleships, gigantic carriers, cruisers equipped for the tropics, proud packs of destroyers.

The bubble of illusions burst on September 3, 1939. Two days previously, Dönitz had submitted a memorandum: three hundred submarines were needed for Germany to fight the British successfully at sea: one hundred in the area of operations, one hundred on their way there and back, one hundred in dock and for training purposes.

In fact, the Greater German Reich had precisely 57 submarines, and only 27 were fit to range the Atlantic. Such were the beginnings of the submarine war against Britain.

IV.

While all hopes hung on the Army and Air Force, while Hitler still believed England would be content merely to wage a "Phony War," the dilemma in the Atlantic could be considered with equanimity. Raeder had no intention of giving the submarine top priority in his naval strategy, and despite protestations, the U-boat building program was making a slower than sluggish start. Dönitz was beside himself: if there was no other way to get things going, he would take over the building program and resign from his post as commander of submarines. His superior dissuaded him: whatever was necessary would be done; Dönitz with his charisma was needed at the front. Raeder was not unreasonable, given the odds against the tiny submarine force. The chief concern of those actually manning the boats at that time, in September 1939, was whether the war would last long enough for them to prove the worth of their weapon. Accustomed as they were to Hitler's "strikes" of recent years, they wondered whether there ever would be a "proper" war. The first British air raid on Wilhelmshaven on September 4 provoked astonishment. Was it for show? Did it demonstrate a will to go to war for real? There was not much destruction, since most of the bombs that were on target turned out to be duds. The whole incident was no more than a prelude. But it enabled Dönitz to impress upon his men that whenever England went to war, she meant to win. They should make no mistake: the war would go on for seven years and everyone would have more than enough of it.

War, the great adventure. While the German Army was rounding up the Poles (who had planned to be in Berlin within a matter of weeks), the Western Front was sunk in boredom: those were the days of the "drôle de guerre," "the phony war"—with nothing going on, not a trace of war fever on either side of the Rhine. Once the two dictators had carved up Poland tidily and irrevocably between them, everybody was asking why the war was still dragging on at all. The Germans seemed to have attained their war aim, while Poland's guarantors—Britain and France—had not lifted a finger and seemed indifferent to their protégé's fate. After October 1939, the war was being waged exclusively by the propaganda machines—and the navies.

In its own way, this was a romantic sort of war: with the big ships penetrating far into the North Sea, with daring raids by destroyers on the British coastline, with steamers captured in tropical waters—and the submarine war. The first wave of U-boats caught the enemy by surprise and scored a number of spectacular successes as a result. A string of names were gaining prominence: Prien, Schulze, Schepke, Schuhart. The last-mentioned had sunk the British aircraft carrier *Courageous* on September 17. The first major sensation came not far behind: On October 14, 1939, Prien penetrated into the Royal Navy's inner sanctum and destroyed a British battleship right inside Scapa Flow. He was rewarded with instant fame and topped the list of submarine heroes who to this day personify the submarine war in the minds of the general public.

But the first successes came accompanied by the first crises. To begin with these were hardly noticed: inexplicable misses, with torpedoes veering downward, or breaking in two, or failing to explode. The German Navy's technical pride and joy—the G7A torpedo with its magnetic detonator and its capacity to cut through the water without making waves—turned out to be an unmitigated technical disaster. For a time, Dönitz was close to despair: it was pointless to give the U-boats any instructions whatsoever and it was downright criminal to send them out to fight with a blunted weapon. The torpedo crisis was to dog the technical war, as its *Menetekel*. In their offices, the designers could see this writing on the wall. Somehow they managed to obviate the defects. The warning was soon forgotten, and the Navy continued to pursue its own romantic war: with courage, with ingenuity, with surprise effects and inspired improvisations. The British and the Americans were more realistic: this war would be won by those with a larger industrial capacity, by whoever could manufacture better arms more rapidly, build aircraft, ships, and tanks in greater numbers. But that in itself was not sufficient:

it was essential to galvanize all the nation's scientific capabilities, to corral all the technical know-how and harness it to the war effort. The Americans came up with the key concept: "operations research."

There was none of that in Germany. Gripped by atavistic racial hubris, the system destroyed Germany's intellectual and scientific wealth. The exodus of talent and of knowledge provoked Goebbels to heights of rabid mockery. Those in charge realized far too late that the spirit was something they desperately needed. During the first years of the war, German science and industry were still nourished by the dividends of the country's previous pre-eminence: Germany had better tanks, better submarines and planes. But development was at a standstill, while the electronic and atomic era was dawning in the United States.

One only needs to look at the lovely ships of the German Navy: marvelous design, a harmonious silhouette, brilliant craftsmanship—and yet, increasingly, they were nothing more than floating toys. They lacked the radar equipment, the targeting mechanisms for firing their guns at night and in fog, they lacked reconnaissance components—the Navy had no spotter planes—while their engines were prone to all manner of afflictions. In 1940 only 57 percent of Germany's destroyers were operational.

And what was the state of the U-boats? In 1942, Dönitz announced that Germany's Type VII-C was the best submarine in the world. That may well have been true, but after 1942 the world that stood at this submarine's cradle went into a faster decline than the sun goes down into the sea. Desperate efforts to keep the antiquated craft fully operational by adding on snorkels, four-gun anti-aircraft batteries, short-wave transmitters, and a better type of torpedo (the *Zaunkönig*) proved totally inadequate after 1943. After years of neglect, the armaments industry tried to work miracles under Dönitz and Speer. New prototypes were developed: A small boat—Type-XXIII—and a larger model—Type-XXI. Dönitz explained to Hitler one day that these boats could travel from Europe to Japan without surfacing.

This new generation of U-boats, which was to inaugurate a "new submarine war," showed—for the last time in World War II—that spark of genius which had been exorcised so ruthlessly since 1933. But miracles failed to materialize; they had to fail because the foundations of science and technology and the resources were gone. Thus the new prototypes were like foundlings encountered in the desert of a Germany ravaged from the air. The Allied bomber squadrons eventually devastated the German submarine shipyards altogether.

In 1939 and 1940 the submarine crews had no idea that such developments lay in store. Casualties were few, fewer than had been anticipated. The record of successes was quite respectable—even though they were not of a kind to determine the outcome of the war. But then, at the time, nobody was expecting anything beyond that. The war was supposed to be won by the Army and the Air Force. The submarines were merely expected—in the jargon of the period—"to make their contribution toward the final victory." The losses which England incurred on account of the submarine war were meant to "explain" to the island kingdom that continuation of the war was no longer a paying proposition, that it would be more sensible to accept Hitler's peace offers before the British Empire was smashed to pieces.

It dawned only slowly on the High Command of the German Navy that the

submarine war should be taken seriously. They too had been persuaded

come of the war. Though even Hitler was persuaded, the consequences were

Such was the rationale for the submarine war from 1943 to 1945, the principal reason for all the suffering and dying of thousands upon thousands of men in the Atlantic, Germany's Dead Sea of World War II.

VI.

Why this failure of the German submarines? Why were they tracked down, hunted, and destroyed without any real hope of defending themselves? In part, German suppositions were correct: the Allies had indeed managed to close the "gap in the air" above the Atlantic; with the discovery of radar they had a device that rendered the submarines helpless. Equally, the submarines did *not* fall victim to treachery: they betrayed themselves through their radio signals. Those in charge in Germany were so loath to believe this that they disregarded numerous indications that there might be a connection. The German High Command could not imagine—and refused seriously to consider the possibility—that the British might be able to tune into the tactically essential minimal signals, lasting no more than a fraction of a second each, by which the U-boats tackling a convoy kept in touch with each other. They would have thought it equally absurd had anyone claimed that the enemy could crack their codes. And yet, the English had managed to do that too. Only many years later, decades after the war had ended, did all this gradually come to light (though much remains obscure to this day)—and hindsight caused people to shake their heads incredulously and ask how anyone could have been so blind back in 1942/43. How was it possible that the radio antennae on enemy vessels had evidently escaped notice? Why had it never dawned on the Germans that their coding equipment had long since yielded its secrets to the Allies?

Defective technical and scientific thinking, inadequate rationalization of the war effort, poor training in the upper echelons, and a good deal of arrogance all contributed to the disaster. The maritime powers had outmaneuvered the German submarine force so that it was no better than scrap iron, but the Germans would not cooperate and would not give in. From then on they were fighting with wooden swords against electronics, but they fought on. As it began to be senseless, the fight became an end in itself.

Senseless: one can argue whether or not the submarine war waged by Dönitz was "senseless" after May 1943. "It would then be a defensive war": Defensive—for what? The Final Victory was no longer mentioned except in propaganda; the real concern was to hold out for as long as possible. But again, for what? Later on, when the war was over and Germany lay in ruins, the explanation came easily: to prevent precisely that. Unconditional surrender, the Casablanca Formula, the Morgenthau Plan, the splitting up of Germany into several states—all these were sufficient reasons to go on fighting until five minutes past zero hour. But there was no way to prevent any of that, once Hitler's much vaunted "totality" of war and hatred boomeranged against Germany. There was no light at the end of the tunnel of war; nothing could be made better by hanging on. Rather, every day the war dragged on brought more ruin, more death, more suffering. Hundreds of thousands died merely for something so abstract as buying time. Not for *Vaterland,* certainly not for fellow *Volk.* Not even for the "Führer," even that was water under the bridge, despite the tone of many a last-minute broadcast from this overrun fortress or that sinking ship.

The Battle of the Atlantic was no longer what it had been. Its aim was no longer to isolate England, to disrupt her lines of maritime communication, to starve her population. Allied ships went back and forth across the Atlantic in ever-increasing numbers. More and more of them arrived safely in England. A huge arsenal of war materials was gradually built up there, which was to descend upon Europe like an avalanche after June 6, 1944. Inconceivable quantities of equipment, of ammunition, tanks, aircraft, and men had been gathered together there—with everything coming from overseas and the submarine war unable to prevent it from coming. Moreover, convoy upon convoy was escorted to Russia besides, so that Murmansk and Arkhangelsk became the major junctions between the Western and the Eastern fronts. The Germans struggled desperately to put a stop at least to that, but they simply did not have the planes; those they had were too few and too old. They never got near the convoys. The submarines, too, were kept at bay; now the predators were the game stalked by Anglo-American "hunter-killer groups." Eventually, the last undamaged battleship was thrown into the fray. It did battle with nothing and was itself attacked and sunk. Men and metal went straight to the bottom. There were only thirty-six survivors.

The situation in the Atlantic was no better; on the contrary, it was even worse. In December 1943, when German destroyers ventured one last time into the Bay of Biscay, they were chased relentlessly by British cruisers. The game was up. Technically inferior, forced by a fuel shortage to cut down on missions and on training, the German force had lost its seamanship. Its seafaring and fighting skills were forgotten. The Navy was reduced to a coastal patrol. The area of operations had shrunk.

Only the submarines still patrolled the Atlantic. But they fared no better. Technically and tactically obsolete, they fell easy prey to Allied escort vessels and especially to enemy aircraft. They were scarcely able to put up any defense. Any successes that came their way were strokes of luck, due less to the capability of the U-boats or of their commanders than to the enemy's occasional mistakes. It is true that the U-boats still had a certain amount of nuisance value. It is true that enemy freighters could have been turned around more quickly and would have spent less time at their moorings if it had been possible to dispense with all the bother of convoys, convoy routes, and wide-ranging Atlantic security arrangements. Dönitz was right, to the extent that everything was slowed down and that enemy resources—aircraft, crews, and ships—were kept tied up in the submarine war. But ever since 1943, the "Anglo-Saxons" had been producing everything it would take to annihilate Hitler's Europe and more besides. Their destructive potential was more than adequate. To keep the war away from the shores of Europe proved to be quite beyond the capabilities of the submarines. Indeed, they could not even act as decoys to prevent a single air attack, because those enemy planes which were guarding the Atlantic and chasing U-boats were not designed to operate over land, except to a very limited degree. Thus the submarines prevented nothing. They did reduce the final score of the enemy's strategic efforts, but to little ultimate effect. The point of sending out a thousand planes on a bombing raid was not so much to attack military targets as to cripple morale. The magic of numbers: a thousand possibilities, a thousand deaths at the hands of a thousand daredevils like "Bomber Harris."

The number of victims claimed by the Atlantic submarine war after May 1943 bears a peculiar relationship to the historical and scholarly interest in the subject of this final phase of the Battle of the Atlantic. Any mention at all of the submarine war immediately conjures up the years from 1939 to 1943. The reason for this is plain: until the latter date, the submarine war was a precisely delineated historical element of calculable import in the overall picture of the war. It was largely subject to rational imperatives and could be dealt with in terms of arguments and counterarguments. But what went on in the Atlantic theater after the autumn of 1943, throughout 1944, and during the early months of 1945 somehow lost its historical coherence, and became devoid of rational interest. Typically, attention was focused entirely on the prospects of submarine construction. The submarine war and submarine production became all but synonymous. It was the Navy's greatest challenge and absorbed all its resources and ambitions. The war out in the world beyond was practically left to continue under its own steam. It was running down, it was supposed to run down, to be overtaken at some point—the following spring, it was hoped at first, or then the following autumn; until in the autumn of 1944, all hopes were pinned on the spring of 1945—by the "new submarine war," which would be "new" because new submarines would herald quite different strategic, operational, and tactical conditions.

In fact, the new submarine war was nothing but a mirage. Throughout World War II, the submarine war remained what it had been from the start, the struggle of the old VII-C boats against the maritime Allies, and death on these boats. The "new submarine" never got beyond minimal beginnings (a number of Type-XXIII boats were deployed off the shores of Great Britain); the successor of the VII-C boat, the Type-XXI, never sank a single gross registered ton of enemy shipping.

If one bears that in mind, it is easy to see how grotesque the unwanted submarine war was, a war whose only purpose was to "bridge the gap" until the new submarine types were ready to take over; a war that was an erratic holdover from the early days of the German offensive, its triumphs become hubris and finally transformed into a nemesis of sheer horror. The Battle of the Atlantic, long since lost, dragged on like a ghostly, senseless, and murderous charade.

One may well ask whether it was not inhuman. But one should not deceive oneself: in wartime, it is all too often human to be inhuman, and our peacetime standards no longer apply. What is more, whoever exchanges peacetime standards most quickly and most completely for the standards of war and destruction has the best chance of becoming a war hero. During the First World War, statesmen and soldiers still argued bitterly about right and wrong, about what was human or inhuman behavior in the context of war. There was none of that during the Second World War—on either side. The problem of unrestrained submarine warfare was no longer a problem of conscience: the submarine war *was* unrestrained and everyone accepted that it was so—until the Nuremberg trials. It therefore seems pointless even to ask whether the German tactics in this submarine war were "inhuman" in the final phase. The moment men are considered resources—"human resources"—it follows logically that these resources will be put to the most effective use without the least compunction; whenever war is measured in the destruction of the greatest possible number of human lives (and after Dresden that lesson was taught again at Hiroshima and Nagasaki), it would be out of character to try and limit the death toll. That death toll is part and parcel of the nature of war.

Most of those doomed to die were never asked at the time whether they wished to sacrifice themselves. The case of the submarine crews was somewhat different: romantically seduced volunteers, it came easy to them to opt for service on the U-boats.

The postwar generation is bemused by this phenomenon, but make no mistake: if today's young people were to find themselves in a similar situation, they would not respond so very differently. The U-boats were not called "iron coffins" for nothing. And yet, until the very end of the war, no direct compulsion was needed to keep the submarines in the Atlantic; indeed, it can be argued that the morale-boosting slogans were superfluous. The spirit of Langemark survived to the end and could be relied on as if it were a calculable military resource.

Those who used that resource acted immorally. The Second World War (including the submarine war) was immoral in just this sense. But that was never dealt with by any tribunal, and the historians have concentrated on other aspects of the war. Maybe it is not a part of their function. Maybe others must help, who saw at first hand the dreadful connection between war, death, heroism, and seduction, and who were able to cast off the leaden shackles imposed on human hearts and senses by this unholy alliance.

When the war was over and Germany had surrendered unconditionally, many U-boats scuttled themselves in accordance with naval tradition—*honi soit qui mal y pense*. About one hundred and fifty boats were left, a sorry remnant of a submarine fleet that had been a thousand strong. They had to hoist black flags and the English led them in single file to their destination. Old scrap iron, of no use to Britain, they were jealously kept from the Russians. "Operation Deadlight" sent them to the bottom of the sea. Finis.

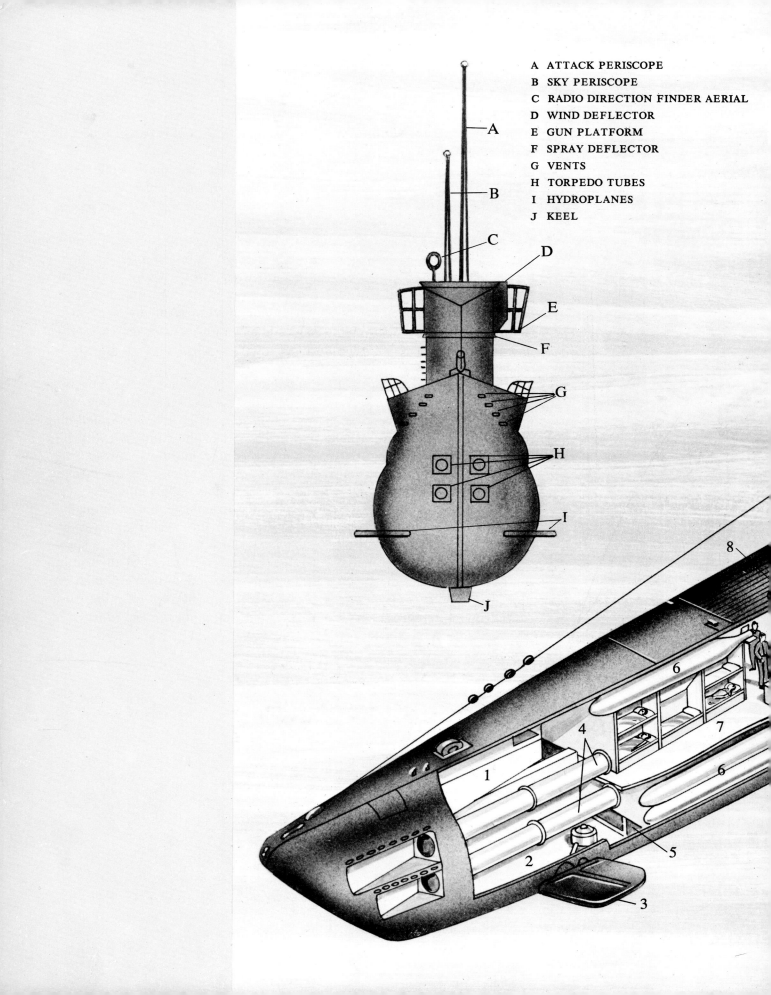

A ATTACK PERISCOPE
B SKY PERISCOPE
C RADIO DIRECTION FINDER AERIAL
D WIND DEFLECTOR
E GUN PLATFORM
F SPRAY DEFLECTOR
G VENTS
H TORPEDO TUBES
I HYDROPLANES
J KEEL

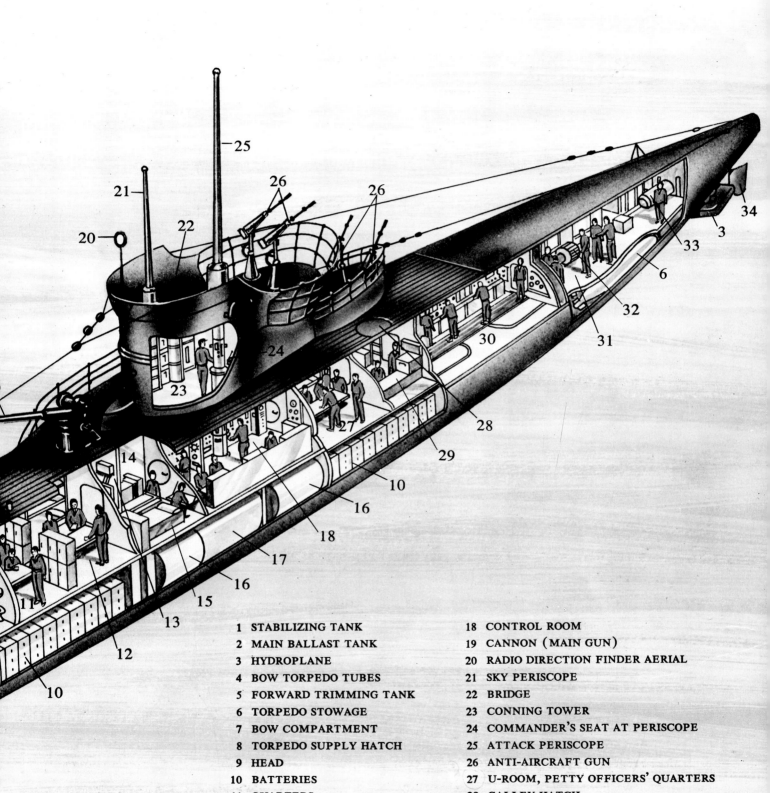

1 STABILIZING TANK	18 CONTROL ROOM
2 MAIN BALLAST TANK	19 CANNON (MAIN GUN)
3 HYDROPLANE	20 RADIO DIRECTION FINDER AERIAL
4 BOW TORPEDO TUBES	21 SKY PERISCOPE
5 FORWARD TRIMMING TANK	22 BRIDGE
6 TORPEDO STOWAGE	23 CONNING TOWER
7 BOW COMPARTMENT	24 COMMANDER'S SEAT AT PERISCOPE
8 TORPEDO SUPPLY HATCH	25 ATTACK PERISCOPE
9 HEAD	26 ANTI-AIRCRAFT GUN
10 BATTERIES	27 U-ROOM, PETTY OFFICERS' QUARTERS
11 QUARTERS	28 GALLEY HATCH
12 WARDROOM, OFFICERS' MESS	29 GALLEY
13 SOUND ROOM	30 ENGINE ROOM (DIESEL)
14 RADIO SHACK	31 MAIN MOTOR ROOM (ELECTRIC)
15 COMMANDER'S QUARTERS	32 E-MOTORS
16 FUEL TANK	33 STERN TORPEDO TUBE
17 MAIN BALLAST TANKS	34 RUDDER

Lothar-Günther Buchheim was born in Weimar in 1918. He grew up in Saxony, and through the influence of his mother, a talented watercolorist, devoted himself to art at a very early age. He was soon recognized as a *Wunderkind* and at fourteen was asked to exhibit his paintings and drawings. While studying at the Dresden Academy of Art, he began work as an illustrator for newspapers and magazines and later joined a master-class in Munich. When war broke out, he joined the Navy, and served as a lieutenant on mine sweepers, destroyers, and submarines—on the last as an official naval correspondent.

After the war he began to collect German Expressionist paintings, and his collection is now one of the most important in the world. He has written several standard works on Expressionism, as well as numerous monographs on Max Beckmann, Klimt, Kandinsky, and Picasso. Mr. Buchheim now lives near Munich.